# The Funniest People in Theater: 250 Anecdotes

David Bruce

Published by David Bruce, 2022.

THE FUNNIEST PEOPLE IN THEATER: 250 ANECDOTES

**First edition. October 8, 2022.**

Copyright © 2022 David Bruce.

ISBN: 979-8215998151

Written by David Bruce.

# Table of Contents

Cover Photograph for *The Funniest People in Theater: 250 Anecdotes*:

Model: Victoria Borodinova

https://pixabay.com/photos/theatre-behind-the-scenes-curtain-3966147/

https://www.instagram.com/victoriaborodinova/

All anecdotes have been retold in my own words to avoid plagiarism.

Anecdotes are usually short humorous stories. Sometimes they are thought-provoking or informative, not amusing.

# Chapter 1: From Absent-Mindedness to Censorship

**Absent-Mindedness**

• As a young actress just starting in show business, Eve Arden quickly learned not to be absent minded. She once finished a play's first act, went to her dressing room, took off her costume and removed her makeup, and then left the theater to take a bus home — only to find the theater manager running after her and yelling, "Second act!" She returned to the stage wearing galoshes and no makeup, where she discovered her fellow actors desperately ad-libbing lines such as "I saw her in the garden, I think" and "She'll probably be here any minute."[1]

• Early in her career, actress Diana Rigg was regarded as something of a kook by her neighbors because she used to lose her keys a few times a year and be forced to gain entry to her apartment by throwing a milk bottle through a window.[2]

**Actors**

• British actor Pete Postlethwaite has a rugged face. When he was studying at the Bristol Old Vic, he ran out of money to pay for the completion of his course of study. However, the head of the school knew that the young man had real talent, so he told him, "Listen, I have a hunch you're going to do all right in this business, so I'm going to put down the outstanding amount as a debt and then, in a few years' time, I'll write it off as a bad debt." Of course, this comment made Mr. Postlethwaite happy, although the next comment did not. The head of the school unfortunately added, "Of course, when you've got a face like a f**king stone archway, you can't go wrong." Mr. Postlethwaite once acted in a play by Restoration playwright William Congreve, and co-star Prunella Scales sent him a telegram praising his performance. According to Mr. Postlethwaite, she wrote that "I was the best Restoration truck driver she'd ever worked with."[3]

• Actress/comedian/writer Ann Randolph got her start in performing when she was hired to work with mental patients at the Athens Mental Health Center while studying theater at Ohio University in Athens, Ohio. One of the activities she did was to write several plays for the patients to perform. Some of the things she saw at the Mental Health Center became part of the plays she wrote. According to Ms. Randolph, "I think it shaped me because I was able to see … how devastating mental illness is. I wanted to immediately tell the stories that I was hearing up there. I wanted to tell them on stage. They were amazing stories." The plays were popular with the patients — one patient even requested, "Don't discharge me until the play is over."[4]

• Carol Burnett made her Broadway debut in the hit *Once Upon a Mattress*, a comic play based upon the children's story "The Princess and the Pea." In this play, her character slept on a bed with several mattresses, under which a pea had been placed. If her character felt the pea, she was a legitimate princess; if her character did not feel the pea, she was not worthy to marry the prince. However, at the same time that Ms. Burnett was starring on Broadway each night, she was also starring on television each day, and she was very, very tired — so one night she fell asleep while lying on the mattresses on stage.[5]

• Jacob P. Adler was a much-respected Yiddish actor who died in 1926. Fourteen years after his death, an old man showed up at a theater where Mr. Adler used to perform. He presented the theater manager with a pass that had been signed by Mr. Adler — but the pass was good for free admission to a Dec. 31, 1919, performance. The old man had been unable to use it in 1919, but he wanted to use it in 1940 because he had heard that Mr. Adler's daughter, Celia, was appearing at the theater. The theater manager had such a high respect for Mr. Adler that he honored the pass.[6]

• Katherine Cornell was a much-loved theatrical actress. Once, she was supposed to appear in Seattle, Washington, but because of bad weather her train did not arrive until almost midnight. Hearing that the audience was still awaiting her arrival, she and her troupe went to the theater and got the stage ready in full view of the audience, allowing them a glimpse of behind-the-curtain activity they had not seen before. Ms. Cornell and her troupe then performed the play, which did not end until 3:45 a.m.[7]

• When Diana Adams first started dancing with the New York City Ballet, like most newcomers she was given the pantomime roles that did not require much if any dancing; unfortunately, she was not much good at pantomime — although as her career proved, she was excellent at dancing. As the Duchess in *Giselle*, she acted regally, but for lack of a better thing to do, looked at the scenery. This amused André Eglevsky, who commented, "That girl, she looks as if she'd never seen a tree before!"[8]

• Actors John Gielgud and Hugh Griffith once attended a party at which Sir John amused everyone by talking of various productions he had seen of Shakespeare's *Tempest*. He especially criticized a particular production, saying it had "quite the worst Caliban I have ever seen." Noticing how quiet Mr. Griffith was, he said, "You're very silent, Hugh." Mr. Griffith replied, "Not as a rule. I was just trying to recall my performance and wondering if you could possibly be right."[9]

• After retiring from gymnastics following the 1972 Olympic Games in Munich, Cathy Rigby began her acting career by playing the role of *Peter Pan* for seven months — traditionally, Peter Pan, a boy, is played by a woman. She is well known for this role, which she has played several times in intervening years. In fact, she says her daughter once told her that "when she grows up, she wants to be a boy just like me."[10]

• Steven Spielberg was looking for an actor to play Oskar Schindler in the movie *Schindler's List* when he and his family saw Irish actor Liam Neeson in the play *Anna Christie*. The mother of Mr. Spielberg's wife, Kate Capshaw, was visibly moved by the play and was crying, so

Mr. Neeson hugged her. Ms. Capshaw later told her husband, "That's exactly what Schindler would have done." Mr. Neeson got the role.[11]

• Actor Patrick Macnee once appeared in a play titled *The Assassin*, whose lead character died in his arms at the end of the play. Playing the assassin was Peter Glenville, who added a few seconds to the death scene each time he played it. After one performance, Mr. Macnee staggered home, collapsed on a couch, then told his wife, "Tonight Peter Glenville took seven minutes to die!"[12]

• Actors and actresses have strange skills. One day, Roger Prout was passing by Elizabeth Vaughan's dressing room, where he heard her coughing and coughing as if she were about to die. Concerned, he asked if he could do anything to help her, but she stopped coughing, smiled, and then said, "It's all right — I was just practicing."[13]

• As a young, impoverished actor, Harry H. Corbett traveled with a troupe in a very old truck. Frequently, the police would order that the truck be repaired in a shop. The mechanics did what they could, but on the bill they would write, "We are no longer responsible for the state of this vehicle."[14]

• Dr. Samuel Johnson could be complimentary when he wanted to be. When he received a visit from the actress Mrs. Siddons, one of his servants was slow in bringing her a chair. Referring to her ability to sell out a theater, Dr. Johnson said, "You see, madam, wherever you go, there are no seats to be had."[15]

**Age**

• Two great Dames of the English theatre — Dame Sybil Thorndike and Dame Edith Evans — appeared together when they were aged. This caused a major problem for the manager of the theater: Which Dame should get the star dressing room? He went to Dame Sybil and explained the problem. The two dressing rooms in question were both very good, but the number two dressing room was at the top of a flight of stairs. Dame Sybil replied, "Well, then, there's no problem.

Dame Edith must have the number one dressing room — I can still climb stairs."[16]

• When Sir Ralph Richardson was 74 years old, Richard Eyre visited him in his dressing room, where he was surprised to see Sir Ralph using makeup to put lines under his eyes, the way young actors do. Sir Ralph noticed the look of surprise on Mr. Eyre's face, so he explained, "Ah, I'm playing an old character, you see."[17]

• When theatrical maven George Abbott was 95 years ago, he had to get a pacemaker. When he asked about its disadvantages, the doctor joked, "You'll have to have a new battery after 10 years." As it happened, when Mr. Abbott was 105 years old, he needed a new battery. Eventually, he died at age 107.[18]

• The last time Leslie Caron saw Fred Astaire was at a benefit for Gene Kelly. A waiter accidentally brushed against her and knocked her off-balance. Mr. Astaire, then 85 years old, immediately grabbed her wrist and steadied her. Ms. Caron told him, "Fred, you haven't lost your grip."[19]

**Agents**

• Diana Adams auditioned for George Balanchine for the Broadway show *Dream with Music*, which would star Vera Zorina, but before the audition her agent told her not to settle for anything less than the second dancing lead. After the audition, Mr. Balanchine told Diana that she had passed the audition and he would hire her. Immediately, she remembered what her agent had told her, and so she told Mr. Balanchine that she wanted the second dancing lead. Mr. Balanchine looked at her and replied, "In this show, there is only one dancing lead."[20]

• Walter Winchell used to write a column that frequently featured one-liners by celebrities; however, publicity agents, not the celebrities, often thought up the one-liners. For a while, one-liners by Alexander Woollcott appeared frequently in Mr. Winchell's column, but eventually Mr. Winchell stopped mentioning Mr. Woollcott's name.

When this happened, Mr. Woollcott sent a message to his publicity agent, Irving Mansfield, and asked, "Dear Irving, whatever happened to my sense of humor?"[21]

• Joe E. Brown was a vaudeville actor for many years, but he played in a star-studded movie version of Shakespeare's *A Midsummer Night's Dream*, a performance for which the movie studio did not want to pay him in money, but instead give him a car. His agent asked, "What would my commission be, a bicycle?"[22]

• Eli Wallach once visited Israel in the company of his wife and his agent. While he was there, a street vendor in Bethlehem pointed to Mr. Wallach's wife and said, "I'll give you 10 sheep and 10 camels for her." Immediately, his agent advised, "Take it — I get 10 percent."[23]

**Alcohol**

• As a young actress, Eve Arden once appeared in a play with Alice Buchanan. One April day, Ms. Buchanan, who was not known to drink, appeared much later than usual to get dressed for her part. Her face was flushed and her speech was slurred, and when she entered her dressing room, she refused to speak to anyone, preferring instead to sing drunkenly. Her friends were sure she was going to lose her job. However, just before show time, she opened the door of her dressing room, told everyone, "April Fool," and then performed brilliantly on stage.[24]

• The 19th-century actor George Frederick Cooke sometimes appeared onstage while drunk. In *Richard III*, he played the Duke of Gloucester, and at one point he staggered across the stage with his sword raised above his head. A member of the audience disliked the performance and shouted, "That's not like the Duke of Gloucester!" Mr. Cooke stopped, faced the audience member, and shouted, "That's not like a British auditor!" The act ended with applause (and a few hisses) for Mr. Cooke.[25]

• An obviously inebriated gentleman came to the Court Theatre to buy a ticket only to be told by the box office attendant that he would not be allowed to buy one. The gentleman asked why not, and the box office attendant pointed out that the gentleman was drunk. Affronted, the gentleman replied, "But of course I'm drunk. Do you think I should come to the Court Theatre if I was sober?"[26]

• Actor John Neville was unhappy in the late 1950s Old Vic production of *Measure for Measure*, so he used to escape to the nearest pub as often as possible. In fact, just before the pub opened at 5:30 p.m., he would lean against the door. When the door was opened, he would fall inside and say, "Sorry I'm late."[27]

• The 19th-century actor O. Smith, née Richard John Smith, knew his craft. In the drama *Peter Bull*, he played a drunkard, and one of his bits of business was to spill a drink, and then throw himself on the floor and lap it up. A poorer actor would have been laughed at.[28]

**Animals**

• The great Shakespearean actor Sir Ralph Richardson had a pet mouse, which he sometimes took for a walk so it could get some exercise. One day, he was walking in a gutter over the mouse — to protect it — when a passing police car stopped to investigate. Sir Ralph explained, "I'm taking my mouse for a walk." The police officer recognized him and offered to use his flashlight so that Mr. Richardson could better see the mouse. For a while, onlookers saw a little parade — the police officer with a flashlight, the mouse captured in the beam of the flashlight, and Sir Ralph Richardson watching over the mouse. Eventually, Sir Ralph felt that his pet mouse had gotten enough exercise, so he put him in his pocket, thanked the police officer, and returned to his hotel.[29]

• William Butler Yeats wrote some plays in the Japanese Noh style, including *The Hawk's Wells*, which created a problem. The stage direction "The Girl gives the cry of the hawk" appears twice, but Yeats, choreographer/dancer Michio Ito, and costume/mask designer Edmund Dulac did not know what the cry of the hawk sounded like. They made a few trips to a zoo, but were they unsuccessful in hearing the cry of a hawk, even though Mr. Dulac prodded a hawk with his umbrella. Finally, they decided that the Japanese word for hawk, *taka*, was onomatopoeic, and so when the Girl gave the cry of the hawk, she cried *taka*.[30]

• Before he became a success, Jack Benny was desperate for work. Hearing that an animal act was needed at a vaudeville theater, he borrowed two Pekinese dogs and showed up to work. However, Mr. Benny simply tied the dogs to some scenery on stage, and then performed his regular act of telling jokes. While paying Mr. Benny his $25 fee, the theater manager remarked that the animal act was very peculiar and asked, "Don't your dogs do any tricks?" Mr. Benny pocketed the money, then replied, "Not at these prices, they don't."[31]

• The part of Nana, the nanny-dog in James M. Barrie's play *Peter Pan*, was based on Luath, Mr. Barrie's Newfoundland dog. To create the costume for Nana, costumers copied Luath's black-and-white coat. For one performance, Luath made an appearance on stage during a curtain call — the audience was delighted. Afterward, Luath was famous and took liberties during his walks at Kensington Gardens. Sometimes, he would even eat buns that he had taken from babies.[32]

• Jack Benny once performed in USO shows in Europe. After a performance one night, he and some other performers were riding back to their quarters on base when an MP ordered them to stop. The jeep didn't stop fast enough for the MP, so he fired some shots into the air. After the jeep had stopped and the MP was inspecting the entertainers' papers, a black cat crossed in front of the jeep. Mr. Benny watched the black cat, then said, "Now he tells us."[33]

• Mrs. Patrick Campbell certainly loved her dog. When a taxi driver accused her dog of making a puddle in the back of his taxi, Mrs. Campbell rose to the defense of her pet by claiming, "I did it!"[34]

**Audiences**

• Marga Gomez, the lesbian author of *Marga Gomez is Pretty, Witty, and Gay*, ran into problems the first time she performed this one-person theatrical piece. Because the piece was new, she placed cheat sheets on the set, out of the sight of the audience. Unfortunately, she accidentally kicked the sheets, mixing them up, and she had to wing the rest of the performance. However, this was not her most terrifying performance. That occurred when she thought Cher was in the audience. All during the performance, she was afraid she would forget her lines. After the performance, she discovered that Cher hadn't been there — just a man who looked like Cher.[35]

• When Eli Wallach was studying to be an actor, he often attended plays (with cheap tickets) in New York. He once watched a play titled *Waiting for Lefty*, which was about a taxi-driver strike. Mr. Wallach sat by a man who looked as if he was a taxi driver and who became very interested in the acting on stage. Eventually, an actor on stage started shouting, "Strike! Strike!" The man next to Mr. Wallach jumped to his feet and started shouting, "Strike! Strike!" Carried away by the emotion beside and in front of him, Mr. Wallach also jumped to his feet and started shouting, "Strike! Strike!" Other members of the audience felt the same way and did the same thing.[36]

• English entertainer Joyce Grenfell ran into a problem while touring in Australia. There, the custom was to buy a box of chocolates and eat them during the second half of an entertainment. Unfortunately, the chocolates were wrapped in crinkly wrappers that made a lot of noise. Ms. Grenville ignored the distraction for two nights, but on the third night she told the audience that if they ate the chocolates after her performance, they could enjoy both her performance and the chocolates, but that if they ate the chocolates now, she would be obliged to cancel her performance. The audience was shocked for a moment, then put away the chocolates.[37]

• In Olsen and Johnson's stage show *Hellzapoppin'*, a gag was that a chorus girl — who had been planted in the audience — would come on stage and "accidentally" step on a blower that would blow her skirt high. During one performance an elderly woman came on stage (Olsen and Johnson used lots of audience participation) and really did accidentally step on the blower. Her reaction to her skirt's flying in the air was immediate: She used her umbrella to beat everybody in sight. The audience roared with laughter, and Olsen and Johnson kept the bit in the show — but they used a cast member to play the part of the elderly woman.[38]

• James J. Davis was Secretary of Labor early in the 20th century. Previous to going into politics, he worked in an opera house, where he appeared in several Shakespearean plays, including *Richard III*. In the scene in which *Richard III* says, "A horse, a horse; my kingdom for a horse," Mr. James and the other young actors were battling mightily on stage, with many shouts of "Hey! Hey!" A man from the audience shouted, "Don't order so much hay, boys, until you see whether he gets the horse or not!"[39]

• Harry Houdini performed many of his escapes behind a screen. He would escape from a seemingly diabolical device quickly, then remain behind the screen and read a book as the members of the audience grew more and more worried about his safety. When the members of the audience started to shout for someone to rescue him, Houdini would emerge from behind the screen, pretending to be exhausted, as if he had been struggling to escape the whole time.[40]

• After a show in Kalamazoo, Michigan, lesbian performance artist Holly Hughes thought that she had "totally bombed." Afterward, a woman who had been in the audience approached her, and Ms. Hughes looked at her hair — her big hair — and again Ms. Hughes thought that she had bombed. But no — the woman had loved her performance and thought that it was the best thing she had seen since *The Love Boat* had been cancelled.[41]

• In 1948, Henry Fonda starred in *Mister Roberts* on Broadway. Opening night was a major success, with the audience members cheering and cheering while standing on their seats. Finally, Mr. Fonda told them, "This is all Tom and Josh [Tom Heggen and Joshua Logan, the authors] wrote for us. If you want, we can start all over again." Later, a critic wrote, "I hung around awhile, hoping they would."[42]

• Ancient Roman audiences did not mind leaving in the middle of a performance of a play if they felt that better entertainment was available elsewhere. During a performance of Terence's *Mother-in-Law*, the audience left to see some performing ropedancers and boxers nearby. When *Mother-in-Law* was produced a second time, the audience left to watch gladiators fight.[43]

• Al Jolson was a huge star. While appearing in the musical *Big Boy*, he once asked the audience, "Do you want me, or do you want the show?" The audience shouted, "We want Al! We want Al!" Therefore, Mr. Jolson let the cast have the night off, and he entertained the audience solo.[44]

• John Barrymore could be temperamental on stage. Mr. Barrymore once grew irritated at an audience that coughed too much, so he flung a fish at it and cried, "Busy yourselves with that, you d*mned walruses, while the rest of us proceed with the play!"[45]

• After watching Eve Ensler perform her play *The Vagina Monologues*, an entranced 70-year-old man told her that he "finally got it." A few weeks later, he brought his girlfriend to the play, and she thanked Ms. Ensler.[46]

**Censorship**

• Jewish actor Zero Mostel was a victim of the blacklist during the McCarthy era. While he was working on *A Funny Thing Happened on the Way to the Forum*, the services of Jerome Robbins, who staged songs, were needed. Mr. Robbins had been a friendly witness in the House Un-American Committee hearings, and people worried that Mr. Mostel might not want to work with Mr. Robbins. But Mr. Mostel said, "We of the left do not blacklist."[47]

• Mae West was often faced with censorship. For example, she wrote and starred in a play titled *Sex*, about a group of prostitutes. As a result, she was arrested, put on trial, found guilty, fined $500, and sentenced to 10 days in prison. Although she wore a prison uniform like the other prisoners, underneath she wore her own silk underwear.[48]

• Ancient Roman playwrights suffered from censorship. For example, they could be put in prison or exiled if they defamed a very important person. However, they figured out a way to avoid punishment and still attack their targets. They set their plays' locations in Greece and made their characters — which were sometimes based on important Romans — Greeks.[49]

# Chapter 2: From Children to Food

**Children**

• Hungarian playwright Ferenc Molnár was very leery of child actors because of an experience that happened during a play staged by Max Reinhardt's Vienna Repertory. The play called for a five-year-old boy who had no lines. Because the part was so easy, the nephew of the stage manager was called into action. Unfortunately, it was a dramatic scene in which one of the characters shouted, and this scared the boy so much that he wet himself on stage. Also unfortunately, the stage was raked (that is, slanted), and the stream of urine began to flow downstage — directly toward the prompter's box, where the prompter was sitting. Of course, the audience members in the high seats were watching the stream of urine, which was clearly visible, and wondering what the prompter would do. Just before the stream of urine reached the prompter's box, the prompter's hand reached out and diverted the urine away from his box.[50]

• While he was in kindergarten, children's book author Tomie DePaola hoped to get the lead role in the class production of *Peter Rabbit*, but because he talked so much, his teacher gave him the minor role of Flopsy instead. In his dancing class, he had learned that when acting on stage, he should react to what the other actors did. Therefore, when the actor playing Peter Rabbit did anything, Flopsy reacted — opening his mouth in shock, waving his arms, putting his hands over his ears. Naturally, all this reacting got a lot of attention and gave the audience pleasure — with the result that Flopsy stole the show. Afterward, Tomie's mother made him apologize to his teacher and to the child playing Peter Rabbit, but Tomie apologized when no one could hear him, because he wasn't very sorry.[51]

• While on tour in Edinburgh, Scotland, John Gielgud played the lead role in *Macbeth*. Unfortunately, he found a matinee of Scottish schoolchildren very difficult, as they giggled during the performance and threw paper cups. However, Mr. Gielgud was astonished when they laughed when his character kissed Lady Macbeth at breakfast. When he made a speech a few days later, he mentioned his astonishment at the laughter, and the next day a letter appeared in *The Scotsman* and explained the laughter: "We do understand Mr. Gielgud's feelings, but perhaps he did not realize that husbands and wives in Scotland do not kiss at breakfast-time."[52]

• During a matinee performance of *Macbeth* at which few people were in the audience, Sir Laurence Olivier noticed a boy sitting in the balcony and decided to give a special performance just for him. Sir Laurence gave a wonderful performance and the entire company followed suit, so that during intermission Sir Laurence said, "That boy will never see anything like this as long as he lives; it's an experience he'll never forget." Unfortunately, when Sir Laurence and the company went back on stage following the intermission, they discovered that the boy had left the theater and gone home.[53]

• Carol Burnett's career got a big boost when she appeared as Princess Winifred in the off-Broadway play *Once upon a Mattress*. However, the play was on the verge of closing after only six weeks. Therefore, Ms. Burnett and other cast members started to picket the theater, urging management to keep the play open. Joining the picket line were several children from the neighborhood. A Broadway columnist figured that Ms. Burnett was paying the children to picket, but after talking to them, he wrote, "I apologize. Carol Burnett is the best-loved girl on Second Avenue."[54]

• When 10-year-old Patricia Fosse started taking dance lessons in the Chicago Academy of Theatre Arts, she was shy and cried at the thought of taking dance lessons alone. Therefore, her parents sent her eight-year-old brother, Bob, along to keep her from feeling alone. Bob Fosse grew up to be a world-famous choreographer for such musicals as *Damn Yankees*, *Sweet Charity*, and *All That Jazz*. In 1973, Mr. Fosse won an Emmy (for Liza Minnelli's *Liza with a Z*), an Oscar (for *Cabaret*), and two Tony Awards (for *Pippin*).[55]

• At a dinner that Alexander Woollcott threw for Mrs. Minnie Fiske, four street urchins followed the proceedings as they looked through a window. They were delighted when Mr. Woollcott and his friends gave them some after-dinner mints, but when Mrs. Fiske offered them some red roses, their leader declined, explaining, "I work in a florist's." Following the dinner, the smallest of the street urchins said, "Thank you, one and all, gentlemen and -women of leisure."[56]

• When British character actress Patricia Routledge was a small child, whenever she would cry, her mother would say, "Have a toffee." Sometimes young Patricia would say she wanted a different kind of candy, but her mother insisted, "Have a toffee." Why? Because it's impossible to both cry and chew a toffee. Young Patricia's attempt to do both would make her mother laugh, and soon young Patricia would laugh.[57]

• Playwright and screenwriter Charles MacArthur used vulgar language and slang around the house, even in front of his children. When Mary, his daughter, was in the fourth grade, she was invited by some other little girls to play a game of "Kick the Can." Mary was "It," and because she didn't know how the game was played, she bent over and waited for the other little girls to kick her.[58]

• When Groucho's first child was born, the Marx Brothers were starring in vaudeville in a comic skit called "Home Again." Upon hearing the news of the birth, Groucho told the audience, "I have just been informed that my wife, Ruth, has made me the father of a six-pound bouncing baby. When the baby stops bouncing, I'll let you know whether it's a boy or a girl."[59]

• Music Hall performer Marie Lloyd once gave money to her dresser to have the dresser's child see her in performance. After all, Ms. Lloyd said, "She mustn't ever say she has never seen Marie Lloyd." After the performance, Ms. Lloyd asked the child what she had thought of the show. The child replied, "You can't dance and you can't sing, and I think you're rotten."[60]

• When Sir Michael Redgrave's daughter Vanessa was born, family friend Sir Laurence Olivier announced to a theatrical audience, "Today a lovely young actress was born."[61]

**Christmas**

• When playwright Lorraine Hansberry was in kindergarten, she received a very nice Christmas present: a white fur coat with matching fur muff. However, she was not pleased by the gift. She knew that although her family was financially well off, other children in their neighborhood were not. In fact, some of the children in the neighborhood were forced to put cardboard in their shoes to keep the snow and ice from coming through the holes in the soles of their shoes. Just as young Lorraine suspected, the other children were jealous of her coat, and they chased her home the first day she wore it and threw mud balls at her.[62]

**Costumes**

• In 1982, Sinead Cusack appeared as Katherine in Shakespeare's *Taming of the Shrew*. For her costume, an exquisite pink silk dress had been designed; however, she felt that the character would not wear anything exquisite. Therefore, she wore boots with the dress, and she suggested to the designer, Bob Crowley, "Let's desecrate it." He agreed, and he said, "Shall I make the first cut?" With a pair of scissors, he cut a slash in the skirt, then she did the same thing. After the desecration, the dress suited the character.[63]

• Born Sarah Francis Frost, Julia Marlowe invented her stage name by taking the last name of Christopher Marlowe and the name of the heroine from a favorite play, *The Hunchback*. Late in the 19th century, she was asked why she didn't act in more modern plays — after all, her finances were being hurt because she preferred to act only in the plays of Shakespeare and other classic dramatists. Ms. Marlowe replied,

"Well, I don't fancy myself in modern drama. I never look well in modern clothes." End of discussion.[64]

• One of Bette Midler's more unusual grand entrances was in a hot dog costume, complete with condiments and bun. At an early fitting of the costume, Ms. Midler ran into trouble. The costumers had used Krazy-Glu in its construction, and because of a lack of air circulation in the costume, the glue had not dried. When Ms. Midler tried to get out of the costume, she couldn't — her hair was glued to the giant hot dog. She was forced to stay inside the giant hot dog until her hairdresser came and cut her out.[65]

• Florenz "Flo" Ziegfeld was a master at making the beautiful women who appeared in his *Follies* even more beautiful. Whenever he inspected a costume, he would turn it inside out to look at its lining. He believed that when the inside of the costume was as beautiful as the outside, the women in his *Follies* felt more beautiful and thus appeared more beautiful.[66]

### Critics

• Robert Benchley was the drama critic for *Life* for several years. He detested *Abie's Irish Rose*, which set a record with 2,327 performances over several years. Unfortunately for Mr. Benchley, *Life* ran capsule reviews of plays previously reviewed, so each week he had to find a new way to write "awful" in his capsule review of the play. After running out of ideas, he began to fill the space with such "reviews" as "There is no letter 'w' in the French alphabet" and "Flying fish are sometimes seen at as great a height as 15 feet" and "In another two or three years, we'll have this play driven out of town" and "Closing soon. (Only fooling.)" Eventually, he held a contest for suggestions to fill the space. Harpo Marx's suggestion was "No worse than a bad cold."[67]

• Billy Rose produced *The Great Magoo*, written by Gene Fowler and Ben Hecht. Unfortunately, the New York critics disliked the play and it soon closed. Mr. Rose, Mr. Fowler, and Mr. Hecht were approached by a few financial backers of the play — financial backers who also happened to be members of organized crime. The financial backers invited the three men to pick any three New York critics they would like to see dead, and the financial backers would see to it their wish turned into reality. Mr. Rose was against bloodshed, Mr. Fowler wanted a few critics to die, and Mr. Hecht wasn't sure one way or the other. Eventually, they decided to let the critics live — a decision that Mr. Hecht later said he sometimes regretted.[68]

• After seeing actress Diana Rigg in a brief nude scene in the play *Abelard and Heloise*, caustic critic John Simon wrote, "Diana Rigg is built like a brick mausoleum with insufficient flying buttresses." The next day, as Ms. Rigg went to the theater, she hoped that no one would recognize her. Fortunately, all of the cast members knew better than to mention the review. After a few weeks, however, she began to think the review funny and soon started quoting it. (By the way, Ms. Rigg knows an actress — not herself — who saw Mr. Simon in a New York restaurant and took the opportunity to dump a plate of potato salad on his head.)[69]

• Robert Benchley was asked to become drama critic for *Life*, a humorous magazine, but he was reluctant to accept the job. Workers at *Life* therefore asked him to stop by and look around. When Mr. Benchley arrived, they shoved him into the critic's office and locked the door. Mr. Benchley worked for *Life* for eight years.[70]

• For years, Percy Hammond was happy as a feared drama critic for the *Chicago Tribune*. Upon being invited to move to New York City and perform criticism upon Broadway productions, he hesitated, saying, "I'm 47, and it is very difficult for me to make new enemies at my time of life."[71]

• Drama critic Robert Benchley once watched a play that used dialect. Mr. Benchley could stand it no longer when these lines were spoken, "Me Nubi. Nubi good girl. Nubi stay?" He stood up to leave, and told his neighbors, "Me Bobby. Bobby bad boy. Bobby go."[72]

• The critics hated Mae West's controversial stage success *Catherine Was Great*. Ms. West commented, "The way the boys wrote up the show, I'm surprised they weren't raided. And to think I took out the stronger lines — on account of Lent."[73]

**Dance**

• Lee Schubert produced the Broadway show *Americana*, which featured some of Doris Humphrey's dances. Mr. Schubert came to a rehearsal, watched for a while, and then said, "Some of the dances are too long. Why can't they be cut down to the high spots?" Ms. Humphrey replied, "Your contract said these dances are to be intact." Later, at a dress rehearsal, Mr. Schubert again said, "Miss Humphrey, too long!" This time, she replied, "Mr. Schubert, please keep your predatory hands off my dances." Mr. Schubert shouted, "I'll see you never have your dances done on Broadway again." She answered, "That will be just fine with me." Then she asked, "Do you know what 'predatory' means?"[74]

• Grover Dale was hired to dance the role of Snowboy on Broadway in *West Side Story*. However, the success of Chita Rivera singing "America" caused a problem for his "Cool" dance, which followed it. Mr. Dale starts the scene doing pushups, and the applause for "America" was so prolonged that instead of doing three or four pushups, he found himself doing 10, then 20, then 30, then 40 pushups. Worried about whether he would have enough energy left to dance, he knew that he had to do something — so he collapsed, seemingly exhausted by the pushups. The audience laughed, and choreographer Jerome Robbins congratulated him afterward on his quick thinking.[75]

• When Simon Robinson became a personal assistant to ballet dancer Rudolf Nureyev, one of the first things he says he learned is that "dance is pain." Mr. Nureyev was dancing in *The King and I* in Cleveland, and a female dancer danced for a few minutes, then exited — and collapsed in great pain. Mr. Robinson came forward to help her, but she told him, "F**k off. Get out of my way." With a great effort, she straightened up, made another entrance, danced a few more minutes, then exited — and staggered to her dressing room. The other dancers paid little attention to her — such a scene was not new to them.[76]

• Onna White was dancing for Michael Kidd when he suggested a series of steps that she thought was too difficult for the "Take Back Your Mink" number in *Guys and Dolls*, so she complained, "That's easy for you to say. You're not wearing high heels." Mr. Kidd asked, "What size shoe do you wear?" Hearing the answer — seven and a half — he put on her high heels and danced the steps perfectly. After that, says Ms. White, "I shut my mouth and never doubted him again."[77]

**Death**

• These are two truths: 1) Divorce can be hard, and 2) The show must go on. Julie Harris was going through a divorce while acting with Eli Wallach in Jean Anouilh's *Mademoiselle Columbe*. For the most part, she did not reveal the stress she was under, but immediately before the curtain went up for a matinee, with tears in her eyes she told Mr. Wallach, "I wish I was dead." With a matinee for the two of them to perform immediately, Mr. Wallach told her, "Julie, listen, we have a matinee. We'll talk about your death later."[78]

• As a young actor, William Gillette appeared in a play in which his performance in the deathbed scene did not satisfy the manager. The manager spoke to Mr. Gillette after the play, saying that Mr. Gillette had laughed although his character was supposed to be dying. Mr. Gillette replied, "At the salary you pay, death is something to be greeted cheerfully."[79]

• In 1848, while the Drury Lane Theater in London was being renovated, a crew knocked down a wall and discovered a hidden room. In the room was a skeleton with a knife stuck between its ribs. Sightings of a ghost have been made several times, but the theater management is proud of its ghost and declines to have an exorcism.[80]

• The great American scoundrel and playwright Wilson Mizner heard about a man in Reno who was executed by means of poison gas. When the warden asked him for his last request, he replied, "A gas mask." Mr. Mizner was shocked that a man with a sense of humor like that could be executed.[81]

• Richard Burbage originated such Shakespearian roles as Hamlet, Lear, Macbeth, Othello, and Richard III. When he died, the clever epitaph on his gravestone stated, "Exit Burbage."[82]

• Lionel Barrymore, who played many, many different roles as an actor, once said that he wanted his epitaph to say this: "Well, I've played everything but a harp."[83]

• George S. Kaufman once told Edna Ferber that he was going to kill himself. Shocked, Ms. Ferber asked, "How?" Mr. Kaufman replied, "With kindness."[84]

**Education**

• Michael Bennett, co-choreographer of *A Chorus Line*, was so disappointed about not being allowed to attend New York City's High School of Performing Arts (because he lived outside the city) that he says he turned his own high school — Hutcheson Central High School for Boys — into that kind of high school. Instead of attending classes, he was allowed to direct and choreograph the high school's productions. According to Mr. Bennett, "They used to send people to the auditorium every morning to see if I was in school."[85]

• As a youth, actor Robert Morley had a housemaster who as punishment would require schoolboys to write out such sentences as "I must not in future pick my nose in class; I must use a handkerchief and never pause to admire the result, but fold it back neatly in my pocket." (Although the housemaster would at first tell the schoolboy to write the sentence 500 times, he would later reduce the required number of sentences.)[86]

**Family**

• Comedian Jerry Lewis was born Joseph Levitch, and both of his parents were professional entertainers: His father sang, and his mother played the piano. At age 15, Jerry began working at the Majestic Hotel in the Catskills. To prepare himself for his job as an entertainer, he developed a record pantomime act. Of course, his parents, who were working elsewhere, were dying to know how their son's act went on opening night, but they didn't want to embarrass their son if things had gone badly. So father Danny decided to disguise his voice and call his son, figuring he could tell by his son's voice how the act had gone over. When Jerry came to the telephone, his father (disguising his voice) told him how much he had liked his act. "Gee, thanks a lot, mister," Jerry replied. "But how can you like my act? I haven't been on yet."[87]

• Comedian Joe E. Brown once learned that his mother was coming to see him work in a burlesque show. Mr. Brown always worked clean, but the other acts were pretty dirty. When Mr. Brown's mother wrote him a letter saying that she would see the show in Detroit, he was ready to collapse because he "knew that two minutes of burlesque would kill her." So Mr. Brown went to his boss, Frank Murphy, and the whole company worked together to clean up the show — which meant pretty much rewriting it. Their effort worked — Mr. Brown's mother was "charmed," and Mr. Brown wrote in his autobiography that "the laughs were just as loud."[88]

• Actress Judi Dench frequently played Juliet in Shakespeare's *Romeo and Juliet*. During the balcony scene, as Romeo stood hidden beneath Juliet's balcony, she recited, "Romeo, Romeo, wherefore art thou Romeo?" An audience member called out, "Down there, Ducks, underneath yer balcony." At a performance that was attended by her parents, when Ms. Dench came to the scene where the Nurse tells her that Tybalt is dead, she recited, "Where is my father and my mother, nurse?" From the audience came the answer, "Here we are, darling. Row H."[89]

• In 1955, Jane Fonda, after finishing her first year at Vassar, performed in a play with her famous father, Henry Fonda. In the play, she was required to enter onto the stage while crying, something that is difficult even for many experienced actors and actresses to do. After performing the scene extremely well, she asked her father, "How'd I do?" Mr. Fonda later said, "She didn't understand that she'd done what many professionals couldn't do in a lifetime."[90]

**Flops**

• Max Beerbohm and Sir Herbert Beerbohm Tree were half-brothers. One day, some friends invited Max to a play, but he was dismayed when he arrived at the theater and discovered that the play was *Hamlet* and that his half-brother was starring in the title role. Max disappeared during the play, and his host eventually found him in a corridor, sleeping on a pile of overcoats. Max apologized, saying, "I always enjoy Herbert's Hamlet this way."[91]

• When performance artist Nicky Paraiso was in his third year at New York University, he played the part of a homicidal maniac in the play *Boy in the Straight-Backed Chair* by Ronald Tavel. As his character killed actors on stage, he could hear his father in the audience telling people, "That's my son! He's the star!"[92]

• One of Orson Welles' rare flops occurred in a spectacular fashion in 1946 when he brought to Broadway the extravaganza *Around the World*, which was based on Jules Verne's novel *Around the World in Forty Days*. Cole Porter wrote the songs, and the musical featured four mechanical elephants, circus interludes, and a cast of 70. Critics disliked it, and Mr. Welles was aware that they disliked it. When one critic said that it had everything but the kitchen sink, Mr. Welles appeared in the next performance with a kitchen sink.[93]

• Actor Sheldon Leonard once left the hit play *Having Wonderful Time* to star in the play *Siege*, but *Siege* flopped, leaving Mr. Leonard out of work. Fortunately, he was not out of work long, because he read in the Personals column of *The New York Times*: "Sheldon, come home. All is forgiven. Cast and crew of *Having Wonderful Time*."[94]

**Food**

• At age 15, Percy Hammond ran away from his home in Cadiz, Ohio, ending up in Washington, D.C., with no money and little chance of employment. Starving, he made his way to the home of Ohio Senator John Sherman, brother of general William Tecumseh Sherman, who burned Atlanta during the Civil War. When Percy arrived at Senator Sherman's door, a butler tried to refuse him admittance, but he cried, "My father and grandfather marched to the sea behind his brother," then fainted. Senator Sherman revived him with food, then helped him find a job as a union printer. Later, Mr. Hammond became a noted theater critic in Chicago and New York.[95]

• Gene Fowler met actress Helen Hayes after he engaged in a drunken revel with her husband, Charlie MacArthur, co-author of the stage play and movie *The Front Page*. Mr. MacArthur brought Mr. Fowler home and woke his wife up to meet him. Unfortunately, when the inebriated Mr. Fowler bent to kiss her hand, he toppled over. "Madam," he said, "I beg your pardon. I grew dizzy for a moment, thinking I was five thousand feet above the canyon, in a high wind. Please charge it off to the Mexican tripe I dined on tonight in Lindy's."[96]

• Ralph Richardson was fastidious concerning the props that appeared on stage with him. In the George Bernard Shaw play *You Never Can Tell*, he carried a silver tray on which was loaded an afternoon tea, including a plateful of biscuits (or, as USAmericans would say, cookies) artistically laid out. At one performance, he said in the wings, "Oh, oh, oh! Celia Bannerman has eaten a biscuit!" His co-actor, Keith Baxter, pointed out that plenty of biscuits were left. Sir Ralph replied, "But the pattern, old fellow, the pattern! It's gone!"[97]

• At age 18, British comic actress Su Pollard was in a restaurant when a man left, leaving behind an untouched pork chop. Because she was hungry, she took the pork chop and ate it — and was both surprised and embarrassed when the man returned after having deposited coins in a parking meter. The man asked a server, "Where's my dinner?" — and Ms. Pollard disappeared into the ladies restroom.[98]

• Oscar Asche used to play Falstaff in the theater. In doing so, he was accustomed to eat an entire fowl on stage and throw the drumsticks at Bardolph, despite eating an excellent dinner before going to the theater.[99]

# Chapter 3: From Friends to Mishaps

**Friends**

• Sometimes, coordinating clothing with one's friends can be difficult. Once, Peter Ustinov invited Wolf Mankowitz to attend a play. When they met to go to the play, Mr. Ustinov was wearing comfortable clothing, but Mr. Mankowitz was dressed up. Then Mr. Mankowitz invited Mr. Ustinov to attend a play. This time when they met to go to the play, Mr. Mankowitz was wearing comfortable clothing, but Mr. Ustinov was dressed up.[100]

• Noël Coward frequently got into arguments with the actors and actresses in his plays, but the arguments were always sorted out later. One day, he and Gertie Lawrence were having a loud argument in a dressing room when a woman in the cast ran into the dressing room and told them, "You must stop this. I love you both and you can't go on like this." Mr. Coward told her, "How dare you interfere when I'm talking with my friend!"[101]

• Betty White, star of *The Golden Girls*, and Carol Channing, star of *Hello, Dolly*, were friends. Once, Ms. White played the lead in *Hello, Dolly* in several Ohio cities, then she teased her friend by saying that everyone felt the production was much better than the original starring Ms. Channing. However, Ms. Channing simply replied, "Your mother said what?"[102]

**Gambling**

• Alexander Woollcott belonged to the Young Men's Upper West Side Thanatopsis and Inside Straight Club, whose members met regularly to play poker. One day, a member of the club brought a rich man to play poker at the club, announcing that the rich man would be easy to pluck. The next morning, Mr. Woollcott and his friends looked up the rich man in Dun and Bradstreet, found that he was worth $60,000,000, then sent that publication this note: "Dear Sirs: He now has $60,000,210."[103]

• The cast and crew of *Peter Pan* were on tour in New England at a time when many people thought that actors and actresses were scandalous. On the train, the actors playing pirates noticed that some scandalized Puritans were staring at them as they played poker (also a no-no), so they seated the child playing Liza at the poker table, gave her some cards, and set some poker chips in front of her. The child gazed intently at the cards.[104]

**Gays and Lesbians**

• Early in her career, Lillian Hellman read and evaluated plays for theatrical producer Herman Shumlin. After she had written her first play, *The Children's Hour*, she left it on his desk with a note saying that this was the best play she had seen while working for him. Mr. Shumlin read her play, agreed with her assessment of it, and produced it on Broadway, where it immediately became a hit after opening on November 20, 1934. Unfortunately, because of the shocking subject matter of the play — a child unjustly accuses two teachers of being lesbians — the Pulitzer Prize Committee did not give it a prize and refused to even consider it for a prize. This infuriated so many New York critics who felt that it was the best play of the season that they formed the Drama Critics Circle and began to present their own awards.[105]

• Charles Nelson Reilly was once invited along with some other actors to ride a float in a Gay Pride parade. All the actors were told that the float would bear a banner saying "Actors for Gay Rights," but when they arrived at the parade, they discovered that the banner actually said "Gay Actors for Human Rights." None of the other actors would get on the float, but Mr. Reilly figured that he looked good in his tuxedo and his toupee, so he rode on the float alone. Eventually, Mr. Reilly announced that he was gay.[106]

• Actress Hermione Gingold once saw a production of *Peter Pan*, starring Joan Greenwood. In the scene in which Peter Pan saves Tinkerbelle's life by asking the audience if they believe in fairies, Ms. Gingold's voice rang out: "Believe in them, darling? I know hundreds of them!"[107]

**Gifts**

• Conductor André Previn has in his office a jack-in-the-box; the puppet that comes out of the box is a conductor. This was a gift to him from British playwright Tom Stoppard. One day, Mr. Previn had told him that he had to fire someone and didn't know how to do it. Later, Mr. Stoppard gave him the jack-in-the-box and said about the puppet conductor, "Just put a note in his little hand, reading, 'You're fired.' Then have the fellow come in and hand it to him."[108]

• Toilet paper can be a much-appreciated gift. At the beginning of World War II, many British people realized that certain products would become rare. English entertainer Joyce Grenfell knew a foresighted woman who ordered a couple of grosses of toilet paper (an enormous order). During the war, she gave it away as presents at Christmas and birthdays to friends who were very pleased to receive the rare product.[109]

• In 1944, Laurence Olivier scored a major success while acting in *Richard III*. John Gielgud welcomed Mr. Olivier into the ranks of the truly great actors by giving him a special gift: the sword that Edmund Kean had used while playing the role of Richard III in the early 1800s. This sword has been passed down from Mr. Kean to Mr. Henry Irving to Mr. Gielgud to Mr. Olivier — truly great actors all.[110]

**Good Deeds**

• At the very beginning of her career, opera singer/actress Grace Moore started touring with a play titled *Town Gossip* that never reached Broadway. Unfortunately, when it closed in Boston no money was left to pay the chorus girls, so they were stranded without a way to get back to New York City. Fortunately, Ms. Moore was able to telephone her wealthy friend Bernard Baruch — she was the type of person who knows many, many famous people — and he paid the chorus girls' way back home. The chorus girls were grateful to him and they paid him back, but slowly — for years afterwards, small checks were sent to Mr. Baruch through Actors' Equity.[111]

• When Carol Burnett was majoring in theater arts at UCLA, she and a fellow student entertained at a party, where she sang songs from the Broadway hit *Annie Get Your Gun*. A man at the party was impressed by what he had heard, and he promised to give them the money to get to Broadway. A few days later, they stopped by the man's office, where he handed them each a check for $1,000 and said, "Use it to get started. I came to this country without a cent. Now I want to show my thanks to America by helping others. Pay me back in five years, if you make it, and someday do the same for someone else."[112]

**Housing**

• One of Jeremy Nichols' friends had a rather nasty experience with the interior decor of a room that was rented to itinerant actors in England. He saw a fur-covered lampshade in his room. Thinking that his landlady had horrible taste, and wondering whether the fur was real, he touched it — only to discover that what looked like fur was a coating of dust, one-half inch thick.[113]

• British actress Hermione Gingold loved the English countryside. How much did she love it? After growing homesick for the English countryside while living in New York, she altered her Park Avenue penthouse — by giving it a thatched roof.[114]

**Husbands and Wives**

• At one point, Lorraine Hansberry's writing of a play seemed to be going nowhere, so she threw the pages into the air, then left the room to get a broom to sweep the pages into the fire. When she returned, she found her husband gathering the pages together and putting them in order. A few days later, he set the pages before her, and she resumed writing the play. In 1959, the New York Drama Critics Circle named the play, *A Raisin in the Sun*, the Best Play of the Year.[115]

• Brian Smedley fell in love with actress Judi Dench and asked her to marry him. She said that she would think about the proposal, then give him her answer, but she never got back to him. Instead, she fell in love with Michael Williams and married him. While visibly pregnant, she was performing in *London Assurance*. Mr. Smedley saw the play, and when it was over, he went to her dressing room, stuck his head in the door, and said, "I take it the answer's no?"[116]

• Ermanno Wolf-Ferrari wrote the comic opera Il *Segreto di Susanna* in 1909. The plot revolves around Susanna's secret, which threatens to tear apart her marriage. Her husband knows that she has a secret, and he suspects the worst, but she insists that she is innocent, and she insists on her privacy. Finally, the audience learns her secret — she smokes cigarettes![117]

• When producer David Merrick's second wife divorced him, she wanted to get a laugh at his expense. She succeeded admirably by taking out this advertisement in *The New York Times*: "NOT RESPONSIBLE FOR ANY DEBTS OTHER THAN MY OWN. [SIGNED] MRS. DAVID MERRICK."[118]

**Insults**

• Near the end of his life, celebrated homosexual wit Quentin Crisp used to give theatrical presentations of *An Evening with Quentin Crisp*. In the first half of the program, he would speak; in the second half, he would answer questions from the audience. A woman once asked him if he believed in reincarnation. Mr. Crisp replied that he did not, and after finding out that the woman did, he asked what she wanted to be reincarnated as. On hearing the answer — she wanted to be reincarnated as herself — he asked, "Lady, have you no ambition?"[119]

• While playing the male lead role in *Romeo and Juliet* in Philadelphia, Charlotte Cushman was insulted when a man in the audience deliberately sneezed in a successful attempt to draw attention from the stage. Ms. Cushman stopped acting, led the actress playing Juliet to the side of the stage, then said, "Some man must put that person out, or I shall do it myself." Ms. Cushman's actions were cheered, and the man was escorted out by several other men.[120]

• George S. Kaufman and the overweight Alexander Woollcott once wrote a play titled *The Dark Tower* together. During rehearsal, an actor who had to wear padding because of his role, said, "I certainly hate to walk out on the stage with a big paunch." Mr. Kaufman replied, "You have grossly insulted Alexander Woollcott." This pleased Mr. Woollcott, until Mr. Kaufman added, "And for that, you will receive a gold medal."[121]

• George Bernard Shaw sent two tickets to the opening night of one of his plays to Sir Winston Churchill, with a note saying, "Please come to my play and bring a friend, if you have one." Sir Winston replied with his own note, saying that he couldn't come to the opening night, but "I'll come to the second night, if you have one."[122]

• After playing Sir Harry Wildair on stage to the audience's delight, actress Peg Woffington told leading man James Quin that she thought that half the audience believed her to be a man. Well knowing of Ms. Woffington's reputation for romantic affairs, Mr. Quin replied, "And the other half knows you are a woman."[123]

• George Bernard Shaw once listened to a very poor violinist. When his hostess asked for his opinion of the violinist's talent, Mr. Shaw said that the violinist reminded him of Ignace Paderewski. The hostess said, "Paderewski? But he's not a violinist!" Mr. Shaw replied, "Exactly."[124]

• John Wilkes was once bored by a conceited young man who told him, "I was born between twelve and one on the first of January. Isn't it strange?" Mr. Wilkes replied, "Not in the slightest. You could only have been conceived on the first of April."[125]

• A photographer once snapped a shot of Noël Coward, then asked, "Could you please tell me your name?" Mr. Coward replied, "I recommend you to *Who's Who* — and h*ll."[126]

**Language**

• In 1913, the widow of Ernest Fenollosa gave Ezra Pound her husband's translations of Japanese Noh plays so that he could make poetic translations of them. Mr. Pound was willing, but he requested help in understanding Noh from Japanese choreographer/dancer Michio Ito, who told him, "Noh is the d*mnedest thing in this world." Mr. Pound replied, "I am only an American. You say Noh is the d*mnedest thing in this world — which means you know more about it than I do. That is why you have to help me." Mr. Ito did help, Mr. Pound did make some poetic translations, and his translations inspired William Butler Yeats to write some plays in the Noh style.[127]

• At one time, Yiddish theater was alive and well in the United States and featured Yiddish translations of classic plays. Anita Loos once was watching *As You Like It* at a free Shakespeare festival in New York's Central Park when an elderly lady got up to leave and asked her for directions to the nearest subway. Ms. Loos asked the woman why she was leaving so early. The elderly woman replied, "I saw it 40 years ago in Yiddish, and frankly, it loses something in translation."[128]

• As a youth, Wilson Mizner decided that he wanted to travel with Dr. Slocum's medicine show. Because Dr. Slocum needed a spieler — a talker who could use Latin phrases to impress the rural customers — Mr. Mizner told him that he knew Latin. He then reeled off a steady stream of Spanish curses and vulgarities that he had learned while in Guatemala. Dr. Slocum said, "By God, you can speak Latin. You're hired."[129]

• English entertainer Joyce Grenfell once spent several months entertaining troops in India and the Middle East. At one place she sang several songs, which were appreciated, but there was total silence — except for a few coughs — during her comic monologues. After the performance, she learned that she had been performing in front of people from Yugoslavia, who couldn't understand English.[130]

• Carl Laemelle fought the motion picture trust in courts of law early in the 20th century. He was out of town when the court made its decision, so he asked his lawyer to wire him the result. Mr. Laemelle's case was decided in his favor, so his lawyer wired him, "JUSTICE HAS TRIUMPHED." Mr. Laemelle wired back, "APPEAL AT ONCE."[131]

• Theatrical maven George Abbott both wrote and directed plays. Therefore, he was very particular about language. When he was in his late 90s, he fell while on a golf course. His wife pleaded, "George! George! Get up, please. Don't just lay there!" Mr. Abbott looked up at his wife and corrected her: "Lie there."[132]

**Mishaps**

• Adrian C. "Cap" Anson was a professional baseball player of the late 19th century. He was also an occasional theatrical actor. At the climax of the baseball play *The Runaway Colt*, Mr. Anson used to hit a baseball into the wings of the stage, run offstage (to first base), then reappear on the other side of the stage and slide into home plate for a game-winning homer. It was an exciting finish, with the actor playing an umpire yelling "SAFE!" as the curtain descended. One day, Mr. Anson ran into a friend of his, professional umpire Tim Hurst, and suggested that he appear on stage with him and play the bit part of the umpire. Umpire Hurst agreed, and that night he stepped on stage to participate in the exciting conclusion of the play. However, once an umpire, always an umpire — when Cap Anson slid into home plate for what was supposed to be the game-winning homer, the ball arrived just ahead of Mr. Anson, and as the stage curtain fell, Umpire Hurst yelled, "YOU'RE OUT!"[133]

• During a theatrical presentation of *Bulldog Drummond*, the villain was supposed to gain possession of a gun, then fire it at Bulldog — but no shot was supposed to fire. Bulldog was supposed to then say,

"My good man, I would scarcely have let you amuse yourself with that toy had I not known it was unloaded." However, one night the villain grabbed the wrong gun, which was loaded with blanks, then shot twice at Bulldog. Real bullets were not used, of course, but the gun sprayed powder onto Bulldog's chest. The actor playing Bulldog couldn't say his line about the gun's being unloaded, and since Bulldog was the hero of the play, he couldn't "die," so he looked at the villain and said, "My good man, you're a d*mned bad shot."[134]

• Problems sometimes arose during Anna Pavlova's tours through the United States. One theater manager proudly displayed a shiny floor that he had specially polished for her performance. Unfortunately, the floor was much too slippery to dance on, so Ms. Pavlova had it roughed up with sandpaper before her performance. On another occasion, it was too late to sandpaper a floor, so the dancers attempted to perform on it despite its slipperiness. Her dancers wet their shoes, hoping for traction, while Ms. Pavlova in desperation poured honey on her shoes in an attempt to make them stick to the floor. Nothing worked. According to dancer H. Algeranoff, "We went down like ninepins ...."[135]

• While performing in the play *Angel Street* in New York, Vincent Price had the misfortune to bite into a well-frozen ice cream treat during intermission, dislodging a cap on a front tooth. Determined that the show must go on, Mr. Price lodged a wad of adhesive tape into the gap in his front teeth, then continued his performance. Unfortunately, the gap of adhesive tape came loose, flying out of his mouth during an impassioned speech and hitting his co-starring actress on her cheek. For the rest of what was supposed to be a stirring scene, Mr. Price lisped his lines.[136]

• When the Cotton Club needed a new house band in 1927, Duke Ellington decided to audition his band for the job. Unfortunately, he didn't have the number of musicians that the Cotton Club required, so he scrambled to add more musicians to his band. This slowed him down, and he and his band arrived for the audition two hours late. No problem. The managing owner of the Cotton Club, Harry Block, also arrived two hours late. Because all of the other bands had already auditioned, the only band Mr. Block heard was Duke Ellington's, and he hired it.[137]

• Ruth St. Denis was accustomed to improvise on stage, and frequently did not memorize the steps of her dances. During her duet with husband Ted Shawn in *Josephine and Hippolyte*, they smiled at each other and talked together throughout the dance. The audience thought they were making love talk at each other; instead, she was saying things such as "Teddy, what do I do next?" Mr. Shawn was saying things such as, "Ruthie, take six steps stage right, turn, look, hold out your arm and I'll come back to tell you what's after that."[138]

• At Stratford, Connecticut, the American Shakespeare Festival participants decided to give previews to high school students. Unfortunately, its staging of *Romeo and Juliet* still had a few kinks to be worked out. For example, when Romeo poisoned himself, he was standing over Juliet, who was lying on a narrow raised bier, and so when Romeo died, he fell over directly on top of Juliet because there was nowhere else to fall. Of course, the audience laughed when Juliet woke up and asked, "Where is my Romeo?"[139]

• Zero Mostel was occasionally forced to deal with mishaps on stage. For example, in a performance of *Fiddler on the Roof*, the house moved every way but the one way it was supposed to move. So Mr. Mostel said in one of Tevye's conversations with God, "Just because I didn't pay the rent to the landlord, you don't have to punish me." And as the stagehands worked to fix the house, he added, "If you were a decent God, you'd put my house in order."[140]

• When Richard Burton was starring at the old Vic in *Hamlet*, John Gielgud stopped by his dressing room after a performance so that they could go out and have supper together. However, Mr. Burton took a long time changing out of his costume so Mr. Gielgud said, "I'll go on ahead. Come when you're better — I mean, when you're ready!" In his book *Acting Shakespeare*, Mr. Gielgud called this one of his favorite theatrical gaffes.[141]

• Actor Esmé Percy had only one eye, the unfortunate result of an attack on him by a Great Dane he had petted. While he was playing a drunken tinker in the final act of *The Lady's Not for Burning*, his glass eye fell out, shocking the other actors. Fortunately, one of the actors recovered himself enough to pick up the glass eye and hand it back to Mr. Percy, who was murmuring, "Don't step on it, for God's sake! They're so expensive!"[142]

• Some anecdotes need not be completely told to be funny; after all, some things are best left to the imagination. In 2007, when playwright Edward Albee was 80 years old, his beloved cat died of cancer. While the cat's grave was being dug, Mr. Albee put the cat in a freezer. He says about his cat, "I put her in plastic and forgot to tell the cleaning ladies. One of them went in there, saw a dead cat and, well ...."[143]

• Fanny Brice was persistent. Once she was singing her big number in a show when her voice cracked — something no one could believe. She made the orchestra begin the song again, and she sang again, and her voice cracked again. So she told the audience, "Just stay in your seats. We'll get it this time." And she did get it, and she received a huge ovation from the audience.[144]

• While acting in a play with Ethel Barrymore, Madeline Lee, who was Jack Gilford's future wife, cut her finger as she sliced lemons in a scene. She brought the lemons to Ms. Barrymore. Ms. Barrymore was supposed to ask for some parsley, but instead, staring at the blood on the plate of lemons, she said, "Go in the garden and get me a plate of blood."[145]

• While performing on Broadway in *My Fair Lady*, British actor Rex Harrison narrowly missed being killed by a huge and heavy piece of scenery that fell to the floor; however, Mr. Harrison ignored the near disaster and continued acting and singing. A stagehand watched Mr. Harrison and then said, "Now I know why the British won the war."[146]

• Early in her career, choreographer Agnes de Mille danced in the play *The Black Crook*. One night, her partner accidentally kicked her and broke her nose. Ms. de Mille reported, "The sound, a kind of wet scrunch, carried to the back of the theater, but, I am proud to say, neither of us missed a step."[147]

• Sir John Gielgud, the actor, was known for a habit of saying absolutely the wrong thing. Once a close friend showed him a newly acquired city apartment. Sir John started off well, complimenting his friend on his sense in moving to town, but he added, "Mind you, I couldn't bear a pokey little place like this."[148]

# Chapter 4: From Money to Rehearsals

**Money**

• Impresario James W. Morrissey once ran low on funds in Galveston, Texas, because the play he was producing was not popular. For a few weeks, it seemed as if his troupe would be unable to leave town because of a lack of money to pay off the hotel bill and to buy train tickets — and to pay the actors their salaries. However, Mr. Morrissey hit on the idea of having his troupe give a singing concert. The concert was well attended, but the audience began to howl when the leading comedian, Owen Fawcett, who did not have a good singing voice, announced that he would recite Shakespeare's "Seven Ages of Men." Fortunately, Mr. Fawcett knew how to control an audience. He waited for the hooting and hollering to die down, then he began an impressive recitation that spellbound the audience. He finished by declaiming, "The last scene of all in this strange, eventful history is second childishness and mere oblivion: sans teeth, sans eyes, sans taste, sans everything — including salary." After that joke, the concert went exceedingly well, and the actors earned enough money to get back home to Broadway.[149]

• Sylvia Miles became an actress because she was incompetent at procuring theatrical props. She was working as a set designer at a Long Island theater when the producer sent her out to get some props. She returned after purchasing the props for $90. This shocked the producer, who told her, "You're not supposed to pay for props. You're supposed to rent or borrow them and give them billing." Ms. Miles, of course, wanted her $90 back, so the producer said, "Tell you what. I'm going to give you a part in the play, and I'll give you $90 to play the part."[150]

• The Marx Brothers flopped in London with a vaudeville skit called "On the Mezzanine." During the skit, the Londoners began to throw pennies on the stage — a deadly insult. Groucho went to the front of the stage, raised his hand for silence, then said, "If you people are going to throw coins, I wish to h*ll you'd throw something more substantial — like shillings or guineas." This joke was quoted throughout London, and the Marx Brothers became successful in London with a different skit titled "Home Again."[151]

• People who provide financial backing for Broadway shows are called "angels," perhaps because they seldom get back their money. Marc Connelly wrote a play based on Roark Bradford's *Ole Man Adam and His Chillun*, and convinced a banker named Rowland Stebbins to put up the money to produce it. Afterwards, Mr. Connelly introduced Mr. Stebbins to a couple of friends, saying, "Meet the sucker!" (Mr. Stebbins wasn't a sucker. Mr. Connelly's play, *The Green Pastures*, was a huge hit and won the Pulitzer Prize.)[152]

• Early in his career, jazz great Duke Ellington was asked to write some songs for a musical. He didn't know that composers often took months to write for a musical, so he stayed up all night writing four songs, and in the morning he took them to the musical's promoter, Jack Robbins, who paid $500 for the songs after pawning his wife's engagement ring. Mr. Robbins then took the musical to Germany, where it played for two years and made him a millionaire.[153]

• Famed theater director Tyrone Guthrie liked to tell this story on himself. He had given an *ex tempore* speech in Vancouver about theater, but because he had just gotten off a plane and was tired, he had not spoken very well. After the speech, a famous Vancouver eccentric, Mrs. Clegg, approached him and said, "I've been sitting here listening to you for the last 45 minutes, and you haven't said anything. I paid $1.50, and I want my $1.50 back." Mr. Guthrie gave her $1.50.[154]

• Sir Barry Jackson once directed an amateur production of Shakespeare's *Twelfth Night* with John Drinkwater as Malvolio. During one outdoor performance, a rainstorm blew up and the audience left en masse, except for a couple of old ladies who remained huddled under an umbrella. Sir Barry hissed to Mr. Drinkwater, "You must go on, or we shall have to repay their money."[155]

• Lee Schubert understood finances. Once, he sold the movie rights to a 10-year-old play and without consulting a contract to refresh his memory knew who had a share in the money thus obtained. One of the sharers was actor Leo Ditrichstein, from whose check Mr. Schubert deducted a few dollars that Mr. Ditrichstein had owed him for several years.[156]

• As a young man, humorous poet Don Marquis worked as a journalist for $18 a week and once turned down a job to work as an actor for $15 a week. He explained later that he had decided to stay in writing because of "the big money." (Actually, he was right — later he wrote a play titled *The Old Soak* that made him $85,000.)[157]

• A man once tried to borrow £5 from Irish playwright Brendan Behan, but Mr. Behan declined to give him the money. The man angrily said that he remembered a time when Mr. Behan had not had even a farthing to his name. Mr. Behan replied, "That may be, but you don't remember it half as well as me."[158]

• Brendan Behan, a notorious Irish playwright and alcoholic, once asked the Bishop of Knaresborough, "What's your f**king business, Mac?" The Bishop replied, "Not as profitable as yours, I'm afraid." Mr. Behan appreciated the reply, and he shook the Bishop's hand.[159]

**Nudity**

• A production of *Bohème* in Hamburg involved nudity. A young woman playing Euphémie, Schaunard's girlfriend, appeared completely nude to model for a picture and donned clothing only when Rodolfo worried that she might catch cold. At a dress rehearsal, things went fine until the nude actress appeared and the members of the orchestra tried to play their instruments in strange positions so they could turn around and look at the nude actress. Of course, this caused havoc with the music. The conductor, Nello Santi, solved this problem by asking the nude actress if she would walk to the end of the stage for a few moments so the members of the orchestra could look at her. She didn't mind, the members of the orchestra got a good look, and then the rest of the rehearsal proceeded smoothly.[160]

• In 2001, actor Anthony Flanagan revealed his naughty bits in a scene in the Royal Shakespeare Company's *A Russian in the Woods*. He says, "It happened right at the end of the play. My character was centre stage, and he was made to drop his trousers so the soldiers could see if he was circumcised. So I spent what felt like three hours — although it was probably about two or three minutes — with my trousers down." The other actors were professionals about it — during rehearsals. However, when the play was acted in front of a real audience, they sometimes made the scene drag on much longer than it should have — especially when the audience included Mr. Flanagan's mother.[161]

**Politics**

• While serving in Parliament at a time when a man named John Robinson was Secretary of the Treasury, playwright Richard Brinsley Sheridan once said that a certain man was corrupting politicians so he could buy their votes. When asked to name the man, Mr. Sheridan replied, "Sir, I shall not name the person. It is an unpleasant and invidious thing to do. But don't suppose that I abstain because there is any difficulty in naming him. I could do that, sir, as easily as you could say 'Jack Robinson.'"[162]

• The famous English actor David Garrick was asked to run for election to Parliament, but he replied, "I prefer to play the part of a great man on the stage than the part of a fool in Parliament."[163]

**Practical Jokes**

• When he was a young man acting in England, Jerome K. Jerome played a practical joke on his friends when they came to see him in a play in which his role was very brief and unremarkable. First, he informed his friends that since he was now a master of makeup and of changing his voice, they would find it difficult to tell who he was on stage. He also told his friends that he had taken a stage name —

but the name he gave them was that of an old actor in his troupe who specialized in playing old men. He then hinted to his friends that in the play his character would be concerned about long-lost children. Finally, he bought a cane similar to that used by the old-man character in the play, and he made sure that his friends saw it. The joke worked. Mr. Jerome's friends thought that the old actor was he, and they applauded the old actor's every move.[164]

• Impressionist George Kirby, an African American, put his talents to use in 1956 when he and several other black entertainers performed in Miami Beach at the Beachcomber. This was during the Jim Crow era, and the *Miami Sun* printed an article with the headline "We Don't Want N*ggers on the Beach!" As the black entertainers were in their dressing rooms nervously preparing for their performance that evening, they heard a mob, including voices that shouted, "Let's get dem n*ggers!" Everyone opened their doors and looked outside, and then they heard the laughter of Mr. Kirby, who had put his talents to use in a practical joke that broke the tension before the performance.[165]

• Some friends played a practical joke on actor Edmund Gurney, who always carried a rolled-up umbrella, even during good weather. The friends filled the umbrella with several small green apples, then waited for rainy weather. The joke played out better than the friends had thought it would. One day, as Mr. Gurney was talking to a lady, it started to rain, and so Mr. Gurney offered her the protection of his umbrella. He opened it over her head, and as Mr. Gurney tells the story, "out fell a ruddy orchard!"[166]

• Theatrical actress Beatrice Lillie enjoyed playing practical jokes. In the 1936 play *The Show is On*, she stood behind a box-office window and co-star Bert Lahr, famous for playing the Cowardly Lion in the movie *The Wizard of Oz*, was supposed to go to her and exchange one-liners. One night, Mr. Lahr approached the box-office window, but she said, "So sorry, box office closed" — then slammed the window in his face.[167]

• While attending UCLA, Nancy Cartwright — the voice of TV's Bart Simpson — worked on theater sets, painting many flats with a thick brown paint that looked like chocolate pudding. One day, she and a fellow student bought some paint brushes, a new bucket, and several packages of chocolate pudding. When their supervisor came in, they were licking the brushes and saying, "Mmmm, pudding!"[168]

• Marc Connelly and Robert Benchley once bought an old horse that was on its way to the glue factory and had it delivered at the house of Charles Butterworth. They took the horse through the front door and into the library, where Mr. Butterworth was reading. Mr. Butterworth looked up and saw his friends and the horse, and said, "Gee, fellows, you've been reading my mind."[169]

• Beatrice Kaufman once asked Alexander Woollcott to write a reference letter so her daughter could attend a certain school. As a practical joke, Mr. Woollcott sent to Mrs. Kaufman what she took to be a carbon copy of his reference letter, which began in this way: "I implore you to accept this unfortunate child and remove her from her shocking environment."[170]

**Prejudice**

• Quentin Crisp, an effeminate homosexual who performed one-man shows in theater, grew up in England, but felt at home in New York, where his eccentricities were accepted. One day, he stood on a corner in New York, waiting for a bus, dressed and made up in his usual manner with scarf, too-tight shoes, fedora, lipstick, rouge, dyed hair — in short, he was definitely an out homosexual. A black man looked at him and said, "Well, my! You've got it all on today!" The black man laughed, but without even a hint of terrorism. When Mr. Crisp had lived in London, people had felt justified in coming up to him, getting close and personal, and hissing, "Who do you think you are?"[171]

• Lorraine Hansberry, author of *A Raisin in the Sun*, experienced racism at first hand when her family moved into an all-white Chicago neighborhood in the late 1930s. Although her family was middle-class

— her father was a physician and an uncle was a professor — mobs surrounded her family's house. At night, her mother stayed awake, patrolling the house with a loaded gun in her hands, and during the day, her father pursued a lawsuit that would give his family their rights. In 1940, he won the lawsuit, *Hansberry v. Lee.*[172]

• Tennessee Williams had a "mammy" (a black nanny) named Ozzie in his house when he was a small boy. He once called Ozzie a "n*gger," and she walked out of the house, never to return. Although his family tried to track her down, they were unable to. Years later, when Mr. Williams became an international-class playwright, he made sure that his contracts stated that his plays could not be performed in segregated theaters.[173]

• George M. Cohan, despite his name, was not Jewish. He once wired for reservations at a fancy hotel in Miami, but the management wired back that they catered to an exclusive clientele — meaning, no Jews allowed. Mr. Cohan wired the management, "APPARENTLY THERE HAS BEEN A MISTAKE ON BOTH SIDES. YOU THOUGHT I WAS JEWISH, AND I THOUGHT YOU WERE GENTLEMEN."[174]

• In the Jim Crow days, the great black comic actor Bert Williams was allowed to stay in a hotel only on condition that he use the service elevator — despite his being one of the most popular comic actors of the day. This saddened Mr. Williams a great deal. He once told Jewish comedian Eddie Cantor, "It wouldn't be so bad, Eddie, if I didn't still hear the applause ringing in my ears."[175]

• Someone once made a remark that George S. Kaufman felt insulted Jews, so Mr. Kaufman rose from his chair and — after speaking sharply to the man — said, "I am now walking away from this table, this room, and this hotel." He then noticed Dorothy Parker, one of whose parents was Jewish, so he added, "And I hope that Mrs. Parker will walk with me — halfway."[176]

• African-American actor/singer Paul Robeson created a critical and popular sensation in his role as the title character in Shakespeare's *Othello*, but he was sometimes forced to cancel his theatrical and musical performances — during the Jim Crow era, because of the color of his skin, he was unable to find in some cities a hotel room to stay in.[177]

**Problem-Solving**

• In Miami, Florida, during a production of a murder mystery play that was set in London, England, an emergency arose that required the presence of Police Captain Ron Finkiewicz, who was in the audience. No one knew what Police Captain Ron Finkiewicz looked like, but rather than interrupt the play to make an announcement from the stage, the female lead put the news into the play. On stage, she asked, "Has Inspector Thorpe left?" Hearing from the other actor that he had left, she then said, "That's a pity. I have a message for him from Police Captain Ron Finkiewicz. His mother-in-law's home was broken into, and she needs to get in touch with him right away." A moment later, Police Captain Ron Finkiewicz jumped up and left to take care of the emergency. Later, he said, "It was so smooth that it took a moment to sink in. All of a sudden it dawned on me. The play was about a murder in London, not Poland. Why would there be someone with a Polish name like mine in it?"[178]

• Tim Hurst was an umpire who enjoyed Broadway theater. Whenever he umpired in Philadelphia, he wanted the game to end quickly so he could take a train to New York and see a Broadway show. Near the end of one game, it looked like he would make his train with time to spare because Philadelphia was leading St. Louis by 11 runs. However, since Jack Powell, the St. Louis pitcher, knew that the game was hopelessly lost, he decided to delay the game so Umpire Hurst would miss his train. Therefore, he deliberately started throwing wild pitches and walking runners. However, once Umpire Hurst realized what Mr. Powell was up to, he allowed Mr. Powell to throw only nine more pitches. No matter where Mr. Powell threw the ball — inside, outside, high, low — Umpire Hurst called the pitch a strike. After quickly completing the game, Umpire Hurst got on the train and went to New York.[179]

• Early Shakespearean actress George Anne (*not* Georgiana) Bellamy knew how to correct an injustice. She had won the role of Cordelia, but suddenly the theatrical management changed its mind and gave another, younger actress the role and substituted her name over Ms. Bellamy's on the playbills. Therefore, Ms. Bellamy secretly ordered some flyers printed up that pointed out that the role had been promised to her. Her servant gave a copy of the flyer to each person who bought a ticket for *King Lear*. When the younger actress walked on stage, the audience called out, "OFF! OFF! WE WANT BELLAMY." Ms. Bellamy, of course, was dressed in the costume of Cordelia and waiting offstage. The audience got the actress it desired, and Ms. Bellamy got the role she desired.[180]

• In 16th-century England, before the establishment of theaters such as the Globe, professional actors sometimes performed plays in such venues as the yard of an inn. However, getting the audience to pay for the performance was sometimes difficult, as people could quickly slip away without paying after the play was finished. Therefore, actors used to perform a play until an exciting point was reached, then stop. After collecting a fee from the members of the audience, the actors continued the performance until its conclusion. Later, after the Globe Theatre had been built, playgoers entered through narrow passageways, which ensured that they entered in single file so they could not avoid paying the entrance fee.[181]

• Dramatic critic Alexander Woollcott owned an island. One day, a group of schoolteachers took a boat to the island and started to have a picnic. This annoyed Mr. Woollcott, so he went to the schoolteachers and denounced them, but they ignored him. Fortunately, one of Mr. Woollcott's invited guests was Harpo Marx, who volunteered to get rid of the schoolteachers. Harpo sneaked down close to the schoolteachers, then suddenly appeared out of the bushes. He was completely naked except for a ribbon in his hair and a fife in his hand. Harpo pretended to be Pan (a god known for his randiness), and very quickly the schoolteachers jumped into their boat and went away.[182]

• Even late in his career, Rudolf Nureyev demanded respect. At the end of a performance of *The King and I* in Cleveland, Ohio, Mr. Nureyev took a curtain call and bowed first to the audience, then to his fellow cast members. Not all of the cast members bowed back. Mr. Nureyev immediately brought his hand down to the level of his crotch — since his back was to the audience, they couldn't see what he was doing — and darted a finger out like a penis for a moment. At the next curtain call, all of the cast members bowed back to him.[183]

• American scoundrel and playwright Wilson Mizner once married a rich society lady; unfortunately, they were incompatible — Mr. Mizner enjoyed spending money, but his wife kept a tight hold on her money. Therefore, Mr. Mizner employed many stratagems to get money from his wife. Once, he convinced his wife that it was a custom to give diamond cuff links to ambassadors who dined at the homes of members of society, then he convinced a bartender-friend to dress up and pretend to be the ambassador from Spain.[184]

• Police make a distinction between high art and low entertainment. In 1922, the New York Vice Police attempted to shut down the *Ziegfeld Follies* because the women in the entertainment didn't wear enough clothing. Therefore, the Follies playbills were immediately altered to include a few blank pages — and small pencils — so that patrons could draw the models the same way that an artist would sketch a model in a studio. The Follies continued to be performed.[185]

• While touring, Anna Pavlova danced on many stages that had broken boards and gaping holes. Her husband, Victor Dandré, began stretching a heavy carpet across such stages and nailing it down, then stagehands drew circles in chalk on the carpet to indicate holes in the stage. This carpet helped prevent many broken bones. A floorboard once broke under Ms. Pavlova as she danced — only the carpet kept her from falling through the stage floor.[186]

• While working on her play *The Autumn Garden*, Lillian Hellman had trouble writing one particular speech. She wrote, rewrote, and rewrote it again, but she couldn't make the speech say what she wanted it to say in the way she wanted it said. Finally, late at night, she went to bed. The next morning, she got up and discovered that her partner, mystery writer Dashiell Hammett, had written the speech for her. It was perfect.[187]

• Unfortunately, people sometimes take their cellular telephones with them to Broadway plays — which are interrupted when the telephones begin ringing. Actor Nathan Lane, while performing on stage in the comedy *A Funny Thing Happened on the Way to the Forum*, used to run off stage when a telephone began ringing in the audience, answer it, and say, "I'm sorry. He's at a Broadway show right now. He can't come to the phone."[188]

**Props**

• Ralph Richardson had an uncanny eye for detail when it came to props on stage — unfortunately, in one case. Judy Campbell performed with him in George Bernard Shaw's *You Never Can Tell*. In one scene, she had to pour tea, and the handle of the teapot was facing the wrong direction, away from her, making it difficult for her to pour the tea. She spoke to the prop man and for the next performance, the teapot was placed correctly on the tray. However, when Sir Ralph put the tray down before her, he said, "Oh, dear. Someone has moved the teapot," then he put the teapot back in its original, incorrect position. Because of Ms. Campbell's respect for Sir Ralph, she didn't say anything about the teapot for the rest of the play's run.[189]

• Famous vaudeville comedian Bobby Clark was seldom recognized unless he was wearing his trademark spectacles — which weren't real, but were merely drawn onto his face. He married a French-speaking woman, and decided to take French at Hollywood High School in order to communicate better with her mother, who didn't speak English. The high school students were putting on a play, and they asked Mr. Clark to take part — as a prop man. Mr. Clark agreed.[190]

**Public Speaking**

• In 1957, character actor A.E. "Matty" Matthews was nearly 90 when he was invited to a party at Pinewood Studios to celebrate British filmmaking. The party went well until one after-dinner speaker droned on and on, boring everyone. Matty stood it as long as he could, then muttered, "Good God, doesn't he know I haven't got long to live?"[191]

• Each night, after the end of her hit play *Catherine Was Great*, Mae West made this famous curtain speech: "I'm glad you like my Catherine. I like her, too. She ruled 30 million people and had 3,000 lovers. I do the best I can in two hours."[192]

**Puns**

• Director Tyrone Guthrie was busy casting *The First Gentleman in New York*. A friend mentioned an English actress whose actor husband was performing in a hit play in New York and who was carrying on an affair with another woman. The friend said that the actress would probably be delighted "to go to New York because her husband has a hit there." Mr. Guthrie replied, "She'll be delighted to go to New York because her husband has a Miss there."[193]

• In England, to "give someone the bird" means to boo them. On the New York opening night of *Bitter Sweet*, Noël Coward walked into Evelyn Laye's dressing room and presented her with a silver box. When she opened the box, a mechanical bird emerged, flapped its wings, and sang. Mr. Coward said, "I wanted to be the first to give you the bird."[194]

**Quakers**

• Alan W. Corson of Plymouth Meeting in Pennsylvania was once told by a shocked fellow Quaker that one of the followers of their religion had gone to the theater, adding, "I have never been within the doors of a playhouse." Mr. Corson replied, "Neither have I; but, I doubt not, many better have."[195]

• At Bootham School, a school for Quakers, the students put on a production of Shakespeare's *Macbeth*. One of the witches fell off the stage, but fortunately the witch was caught and then returned to the stage, where the witch was immediately asked, "Where hast thou been, sister?"[196]

**Rehearsals**

• In the early 1980s, a gay teenager named Aaron Fricke once showed up for a high-school play dress rehearsal wearing fishnet stockings, an Afro wig, a corset, high heels, and a black cape, even though he was playing the role of a straight cabdriver. His outfit bothered no one — including his drama teacher.[197]

• Peter Ustinov was habitually late for rehearsals. By accident, he once arrived 10 minutes early for a rehearsal. Sir Peter immediately apologized to the director, Denis Carey, "I'm sorry, Denis. Utterly unforgivable. I assure you such a careless mistake will never happen again." Mr. Carey said later, "It didn't."[198]

• At Michigan State University, a rehearsal of Eve Ensler's *Vagina Monologues* took place in a room next to a history conference. Participants in the conference heard an actress shouting her lines:

"C*NT! C*NT!

"SAY IT! SAY IT!

"C*NT! C*NT!

"SAY IT! SAY IT!"[199]

# Chapter 5: From Religion to Writing

**Religion**

• Humorist Robert Benchley, who was also a theater critic, once heard that no horses had ever been in Venice, which is renowned for its canals. Therefore, when he went on a trip to Europe, including a stop in Venice, he carried a suitcase of horse droppings. Very early in the morning, he went to the Piazza of St. Mark and placed the horse droppings at intervals chosen to be extremely natural. According to Mr. Benchley's friend, Charles MacArthur, "The Venetians consider the horse droppings the only miracle of the 20th century."[200]

• Rabbi Abraham Isaac Kook was once asked why he had not opposed the building of theaters in Israel. After all, according to the Talmud, "He who frequents circuses and theaters has no share in the world to come." Rabbi Kook replied, "There is another passage in the Talmud that says that in the world to come, all the theaters will be converted into synagogues. The more theaters now, the more synagogues then."[201]

**Revenge**

• Satirist Stan Freberg had major difficulties with producer David Merrick while trying to turn his record album *Stan Freberg Presents the United States of America* into a Broadway musical. In the end, it never did make it to Broadway. One of the works of art in Mr. Freberg's house is a bird cage in which sits a papier-mâché bird (created by Kim Stussy) bearing a marked resemblance to Mr. Merrick. Underneath the bird is not a newspaper, but a photograph of Mr. Merrick.[202]

• A young actor grew tired of having just one line to speak in Shakespeare's *Macbeth* — he played the messenger who tells Macbeth, "My Lord, the queen is dead," and then walks offstage. Therefore, he asked his boss, Sir Donald Wolfit, for a bigger part. However, Sir Donald declined to give him a better part, so the actor decided to get revenge. At the next performance of *Macbeth*, he walked on stage and said, "My Lord, the queen is much better and is even now at dinner."[203]

**Royalty**

• James M. Barrie once attended a birthday party for three-year-old Princess Margaret Rose, the daughter of King George VI and Queen Elizabeth of England. About her favorite present, Mr. Barrie asked, "Is that your very own?" Princess Margaret immediately placed it between Mr. Barrie and herself, and said, "It is yours — and mine." Later, the princess said about Mr. Barrie, "I know that man. He is my greatest friend — and I am his greatest friend." At the princess' birthday party, she spoke some words that Mr. Barrie liked so much that he told her that they would appear in his next play. In addition, he told her that he would pay her a royalty of a penny each time the character spoke her words on stage. Later, King George VI wrote Mr. Barrie and joked that unless he paid the princess her royalties, he would have his lawyers contact him. Mr. Barrie immediately set about acquiring a bag of bright new pennies to present to the princess.[204]

• The British have the reputation of NOT being a passionate people, unlike the French and Spanish. Once while Tallulah Bankhead was shown her suite at a hotel, she was told that the Duke and Duchess of Windsor had spent their honeymoon there. Ms. Bankhead felt the bed, then said, "Ah yes, it's still cold."[205]

**Sex**

• At the very beginning of her career, opera singer/actress Grace Moore made the rounds of booking offices, hoping for a job on Broadway. One of the men in charge of casting looked her over, then said, "The voice may be okay, but lift your skirt, girlie, so I can see your legs." She slapped him, then made her exit as she told him, "I don't sing with my legs." In her autobiography, *You're Only Human Once*, Ms. Moore later wrote, "Managers seemed never to consider the voice as a separate entity from what went on below."[206]

• In England, a vicar was on a train with a bunch of actresses who were going to perform in the pantomime *Dick Whittington*. He gave them pieces of the lemon-flavored hard candy known as acid drops, then began to ask them about the parts they would perform. He asked one actress, "Which part do you take?" She answered, "The cat." Eventually, he asked, "And which of you takes Dick?" One actress, annoyed by the persistent questioning, replied, "We all do, dear, but not for acid drops."[207]

• Lesbian playwright Holly Hughes had a very good reason for writing plays — to get girls. She would write a play that starred the girl she was pursuing. Of course, Ms. Hughes would play the love interest of the star. In her introduction to *Dress Suits for Hire*, Ms. Hughes writes about the difficulty of writing a commissioned play for some people she knew she would not sleep with: "It was hard for me to imagine why someone would go to all the work to write a play if there was absolutely no chance she would get laid as a result. What was the point?"[208]

• Edna Ferber and George Kaufman did much of their writing in Ms. Ferber's room at the Hotel Algonquin while they collaborated on the play *Dinner at Eight*. The owner and manager of the hotel was Frank Case, who permitted as little hanky-panky as possible at the hotel. Once, very early in the morning, he telephoned Ms. Ferber and asked, "Do you have a gentleman in your room?" She replied, "I don't know. Wait a minute, and I'll ask him."[209]

• When the future Mrs. Zero Mostel was touring as a chorus girl in vaudeville, she noticed that one particular girl in the chorus — seventh girl from the left — dated trombone players. Never any other kind of musician — just trombone players. Eventually, she discovered why. The vaudeville show traveled with its own music, and on the music for the trombone was handwritten this note: "Seventh from the left f**ks."[210]

• During the "Popish terror" of 1681, English citizens were very angry at Catholics. Thinking that actress Nell Gwyn was King Charles II's Catholic mistress, they surrounded her carriage, but she was able to save herself by pointing out, correctly, "Good people, let me pass. I am the *Protestant* whore."[211]

• British actor Pitt Wilkinson once walked into the kitchen of his boarding house, only to discover his landlady on top of the kitchen table having sex with the milkman. She looked at him and calmly said, "I bet you think I'm a right flirt, don't you?"[212]

• Comte Robert de Montesquiou, a cultured homosexual, fell so deeply in love with actress Sarah Bernhardt that he had sex with her. Big mistake. The only heterosexual sex that he had in his life made him feel ill for an entire day.[213]

**Shakespeare**

• As a student at Eton, Patrick Macnee was cast as Macduff in a performance of *Macbeth*. Playing Lady Macbeth was a young boy named Simon Phipps. Unfortunately, the wardrobe woman made a mistake when she designed young Simon's costume — she used a couple of pieces of metal to give Lady Macbeth a 38-inch bust. Young Simon's appearance as Lady Macbeth was punctuated with wolf whistles from the all-male audience. Reviews of the play stated that Mr. Macnee didn't seem to know what to do with his hands, so a friend suggested that he should have grabbed Lady Macbeth.[214]

• H. Chance Newton used to tell a story about a cousin of his who was suddenly called on to play the part of Osric in *Hamlet*. Being unfamiliar with the part, he put a copy of the play in Osric's hat, planning to look up his dialogue as needed. Unfortunately, he came across a word he was unfamiliar with and hesitated during a speech. An audience member in the balcony, who had been observing the actor reading the copy of the play hidden in his hat, called out, "SPELL IT, OLD PAL! WE'LL TELL YOU WHAT IT IS!"[215]

• In *Macbeth*, the character of Lady Macbeth disappears between the banquet scene in the middle of Act 3 and the sleepwalking scene at the beginning of act 5. Because of this long absence from the stage, some very good actresses have declined to play Lady Macbeth. For example, Edith Evans would not play Lady Macbeth because, she explained, the play has "a page missing."[216]

• Drama critic Sheridan Morley remembers overhearing an interesting conversation at a performance of Shakespeare's *Antony and Cleopatra*. At the end of the play, the stage was strewn with dead characters. As the curtain slowly dropped, hiding the corpses, Mr. Morley heard a woman telling her friend, "The very same thing, dear, happened to Maureen."[217]

• Sinead Cusack prepares physically for her roles in Shakespeare. Because she feels that Beatrice in *Much Ado About Nothing* is graceful with "fluid" movements, she learned to dance before playing the role. And because she thinks Katherine in *The Taming of the Shrew* has "jagged" movements, she pumped iron before playing that role.[218]

• After playing King Lear, Sir Henry Irving made his bows and spoke a few words to the audience. A member of the audience shouted, "Why didn't you speak like that before?" Mystified, Sir Henry turned to actress Ellen Terry, who told him that all during the play she had not been able to understand anything he had said.[219]

• While preparing a wall for his stage production of *Romeo and Juliet*, realist director Franco Zeffirelli flicked a brush soaked with dirty and watery paint about 18 inches from the bottom of the wall, explaining, "This is where the dogs pee." He then flicked the brush higher on the wall, adding, "and this is where the men pee."[220]

• Lesbian comedian Sara Cytron was a class clown. To get her to be quiet during class, her English teacher used to give her five minutes at the beginning of class to recite any Shakespeare monologue in any accent she chose. Her favorite was a monologue featuring Lady Macbeth speaking with a Brooklyn accent.[221]

• Vaudeville comedian Bobby Clark did not believe in the classics. For example, he thought that Lady Macbeth's sleep-walking scene could be considerably enlivened if the director would put a carnival air blower under her skirts so that they would rise up as do Marilyn Monroe's in the movie *The Seven Year Itch*.[222]

• The 19th-century actor Edwin Booth once gave a performance of *King Lear* in a mosquito-infested theater. On stage as King Lear, he asked the character Edgar, "What is your study?" Edgar replied, "How to prevent the fiend, and to kill vermin." Mr. Booth then interpolated, "Skeeters an' sich?"[223]

• While in high school, African-American actor/singer Paul Robeson played Mark Antony in Shakespeare's *Julius Caesar*. The play was much talked about by the students — because the student playing Caesar used lots of ketchup to represent blood in the assassination scene.[224]

• Barbara Feldon, the beautiful Agent 99 on the 1960s TV series *Get Smart*, is very intelligent. After graduating from Carnegie Tech Drama School, she appeared on the quiz show *The $64,000 Question*, where she won the top prize by answering a question about King Lear.[225]

• Diana Rigg once played Cordelia to Paul Scofield's King Lear. After she recited, "Had you not been their father, these white flakes did challenge pity of them," Mr. Scofield murmured, "Are you suggesting I've got dandruff?"[226]

**Stages**

• Comedian Joey Adams was once part of a troupe that was presenting *Tobacco Road* at a hotel in the Catskills. For hours, the troupe worked on the stage, getting it just right and carrying in mounds of dirt, small trees, vines and bushes, and everything else it took to make a completely naturalistic stage setting. Finally, everything was perfect, and the troupe went off to relax before the show. When they returned to the stage, every tree, every bush, every vine, and every lump of dirt was gone. The owner of the hotel had walked in, seen the stage setting, figured that one of his rivals was trying to sabotage the new show, and ordered everything cleaned up.[227]

• Dancing can be strenuous. At the University of North Carolina at Chapel Hill, dance critic Walter Terry practiced dance with Marion Tatum, who frequently tore the soles of her feet practicing fouettés. Twenty years after leaving UNC, Mr. Terry returned to the stage where he and Ms. Tatum used to practice — and her bloodstains were still on the floor.[228]

**Telegrams**

• Eddie Cantor says that Fanny Brice loved to play cards, but that she took an extraordinarily long time to decide which card to discard. Anyone who played cards with her had to wait and wait and wait for her turn to end. (Occasionally, they would break the monotony of waiting by saying to Ms. Brice, "Well?") One day Mr. Cantor was playing cards with her when he excused himself, left her hotel, went to the train station, took one train to Chicago, then another train to New York City. In New York City, he sent her a telegram: "WELL?"[229]

• After *The Mary Tyler Moore Show* ended, Ms. Moore performed on Broadway in *Whose Life is It, Anyway?* Although Ms. Moore had trained herself as a dancer, her role was that of a quadriplegic, meaning that she had to hold her body still and act with only her face and voice. Ed Asner (who played the character Lou Grant in *The Mary Tyler Moore Show*) sent her this telegram: "NICE TO KNOW ALL THOSE DANCING LESSONS HAVE PAID OFF AT LAST."[230]

• Theatrical producer Florenz "Flo" Ziegfeld sent many long, expensive telegrams to the people who worked for him, people he wanted to work for him, and people in general. Sometimes, a telegram would be five pages long! Despite the excessive length of many of his telegrams, Mr. Ziegfeld often ended them with this note: "DETAILS WILL FOLLOW LATER."[231]

• Comedian Beatrice Lillie became good friends with a young woman named Ellen Graham. One day, the two said a very long goodbye on the telephone. Two hours later as Ms. Graham boarded her plane, the stewardess gave her a telegram from Ms. Lillie. It said: "WHY HAVEN'T YOU WRITTEN?"[232]

• An accident on stage resulted in the amputation of one of Sarah Bernhardt's legs. Shortly after the amputation, she received a telegram offering her $100,000 if she would allow her leg to be put on display at the Pan-American Exhibition in San Francisco. She sent back this telegram: "WHICH LEG?"[233]

• Playwright Rachel Crothers once received this telegram from a producer: "SEND SCRIPT AND IF GOOD WILL SEND CHECK." She telegraphed this message in reply: "SEND CHECK AND IF GOOD WILL SEND SCRIPT."[234]

**Tickets**

• One day, Hungarian playwright Ferenc Molnár and a friend attended a play as a guest of the management. Unfortunately, the play was very bad, and so Mr. Molnár stood up to leave. But his friend stopped him, reminding him that as guests, they were obligated to stay until the end of the performance. Mr. Molnár sat down for a little while, then stood up again. His friend asked, "Where are you going?" Mr. Molnár replied, "I'm going to the box office to buy two tickets so we can leave."[235]

• Playwright John Mortimer once stopped for gasoline at a station near Covent Garden. The attendant pumping his gas recognized him, saying that he had sat near Mr. Mortimer at a performance of the opera *Aida*. This surprised Mr. Mortimer, as those seats were very expensive, so he asked the gas station attendant how he could afford the tickets. The attendant explained that he hadn't spent any more for the tickets than any other pump man would spend getting drunk Friday night.[236]

**Travel**

• Declan Donnellan, co-director of *Cheek by Jowl*, has directed Shakespeare around the world. In Uruguay, he directed the balcony scene of *Romeo and Juliet* in a real orange grove with a real balcony. In Sri Lanka, Romeo and Juliet came from different backgrounds: he spoke Sinhalese and she spoke Tamil. In Katmandu, he held a workshop on the *deus ex machina* in *Pericles* and realized that the king's son — who was himself regarded as a god — was present. In Warsaw, he wasn't able to do a workshop on Shakespeare because the photocopier was confiscated on the basis of its being an illegal press.[237]

• Fanny Brice showed she could take care of herself in her early attempts at show business. Many vaudeville comedians used to tell stories of traveling with shows whose managers skipped with the funds, leaving the comedians stranded far from home. Fanny's story is somewhat different. When her show's manager tried to skip with the funds, Fanny followed the manager to the train station and forced the manager to buy her a ticket home. Fanny's response to this unfortunate closing of her show? "Now — I'll find another show."[238]

• While traveling in the Soviet Union in 1939, Noël Coward stayed at a Leningrad hotel where he turned on the tap and was shocked to discover tadpoles coming out along with the water. He complained to the hotel's management, saying, "In England, when we want hot water, we turn on the tap marked 'Hot.' When we want cold water, we turn on the tap marked 'Cold.' And when we want tadpoles, we turn on the tap marked 'Tadpoles.'"[239]

**Work**

• When Jerome Robbins decided to devote himself to dance, his parents opposed him. They strongly preferred that he choose a different occupation — even shoe making — and they sent him to talk to various relatives in an attempt to bring him to his senses. However, he declined to give up his ambition, and he even scrubbed floors at times to pay his dance tuition. Later, he became world famous as the choreographer of

*On the Town, The King and I, Peter Pan, West Side Story, Gypsy, A Funny Thing Happened on the Way to the Forum,* and *Fiddler on the Roof.*[240]

• English entertainer Joyce Grenfell had a problem with amateurs stealing her material. Frequently, she received letters from people asking for copies of her sketches so that they could perform them before other people. Of course, as an entertainer, she made her living by performing that material, and so she used to write back, suggesting as kindly as possible that the amateur ought to write her own original material.[241]

• Frederic Norton wrote the music for the successful British production *Chu Chin Chow.* After the show had ended, Mr. Norton went to the income tax office and asked how much he owed. The income tax man told him, Mr. Norton wrote a check, and as he handed the check over, he said, "It's the last you will get because I am never going to work again." True to his word, Mr. Norton never worked again.[242]

• Choreographer Michael Bennett used to say, "Go with the talent," although Tommy Tune worried that this advice could lead to "a chorus of misfits." Nevertheless, Mr. Tune was grateful to Mr. Bennett for hiring him to be a member of a chorus. At one end of the chorus line was six-foot-six-and-a-half-inch Tommy Tune; at the other end was four-foot-eleven-inch Baayork Lee.[243]

• Playwright Ferenc Molnar customarily slept late in the morning. One day, he was forced to rise early so he could serve as a witness at a court case. Standing outside his door, he was astonished at the hustle and bustle of people going about their business. "Great heavens!" he said. "Are all these people witnesses in this fool case?"[244]

• Actor Hans Conried, a very talented actor with a very long resume, once went to a meeting with a young producer who didn't even take his feet off his desk when Mr. Conried entered his office. The young producer said, "Well, Mr. Conried, tell me what you've done." Mr. Conried looked at him and said, "You first."[245]

• Whenever playwright Eugene O'Neill wished not to be disturbed, he used to hang this sign on his door: "Go to h*ll."[246]

**Writing**

• Irish playwright Brendan Behan once collapsed on the street and was taken to a doctor, who gave him a cardiograph. As the needle of the cardiograph traced out on paper Mr. Behan's faint heartbeat, the doctor joked that this was very likely the most important writing that the famous playwright had ever done. Mr. Behan replied, "Aye, and it's straight from the heart, too."[247]

• Richard Brinsley Sheridan took a long time to write the final scene of his play *The Critic*. In fact, he still had not written it two days before the play was to open. Finally, friends locked him in a room with a supply of food and drink and refused to let him out until he had finished writing the scene.[248]

• Following a stint as a playwright, Wilson Mizner became a Hollywood scriptwriter. One day, he told a plot to a producer, who said it had no audience appeal. Mr. Mizner replied, "The tale I just told you was *The Deep Purple*. It ran for two years on Broadway, and I wrote it."[249]

• After becoming famous for his G-rated stories about growing up, Sam Levenson was the victim of a *bon mot* by George S. Kaufman. Three little old ladies were walking down the street. Mr. Kaufman saw them and said, "Here come Sam Levenson's writers."[250]

# Appendix A: Bibliography

Adams, Franklin P., et. al. *Percy Hammond: A Symposium in Tribute*. Garden City, NY: Doubleday, Doran & Co., Inc., 1936.

Adams, Joey. *The Borscht Belt*. With Henry Tobias. New York: Avon Books, 1966.

Adler, Bill. *Jewish Wit and Wisdom*. New York: Dell Publishing Co., Inc, 1969.

Allen, Everett S. *Famous American Humorous Poets*. New York: Dodd, Mead & Company, 1968.

Aller, Susan Bivin. *J.M. Barrie: The Magic Behind Peter Pan*. Minneapolis, MN: Lerner Publications Company, 1994.

Allison, Amy. *Shakespeare's Globe*. San Diego, CA: Lucent Books, 2000.

Arden, Eve. *Three Phases of Eve: An Autobiography*. New York: St. Martin's Press, 1985.

Bailey, Paul, editor. *The Stately Homo: A Celebration of the Life of Quentin Crisp*. London: Bantam Press, 2000.

Banks, Morwenna, and Amanda Swift. *The Joke's on Us: Women in Comedy from Music Hall to the Present Day*. London: Pandora Press, 1987.

Benchley, Nathaniel. *Robert Benchley*. New York: McGraw-Hill Book Company, Inc., 1955.

Benson, Constance. *Mainly Players: Bensonian Memories*. London: Thornton Butterworth, Ltd., 1926.

Berry, Ralph, compiler and editor. *The Methuen Book of Shakespeare Anecdotes*. London: Methuen Drama, 1992.

Berry, Ralph. *On Directing Shakespeare*. London: Hamish Hamilton, 1989.

Boxer, Tim. *The Jewish Celebrity Hall of Fame*. New York: Shapolsky Publishers, 1987.

Brandreth, Gyles. *Great Theatrical Disasters*. New York: St. Martin's Press, 1982.

Brown, David. *Star Billing: Tell-Tale Trivia from Hollywood*. London: Weidenfeld and Nicolson, Limited, 1985.

Brown, Joe E. *Laughter is a Wonderful Thing*. As told to Ralph Hancock. New York: A.S. Barnes and Co., 1956.

Brown, Michèle and Ann O'Connor. *Hammer and Tongues: A Dictionary of Women's Wit and Humour*. London: J.M. Dent and Sons, Ltd., 1986.

Bryan III, J. *Merry Gentlemen (and One Lady)*. New York: Atheneum, 1985.

Burke, John. *Rogue's Progress: The Fabulous Adventures of Wilson Mizner*. New York: G.P. Putnam's Sons, 1975.

Burton, Hal, editor. Acting in the Sixties. London: British Broadcasting Corporation, 1970.

Caldwell, Helen. *Michio Ito: The Dancer and His Dances*. Berkeley, CA: University of California Press, 1977.

Cantor, Eddie. *As I Remember Them*. New York: Duell, Sloan and Pearce, 1963. (Mr. Cantor's collaborator for most of these pieces was Vivian M. Bowes, to whom he gives credit on the acknowledgements page.)

Cartwright, Nancy. *My Life as a 10-Year-Old Boy*. New York: Hyperion, 2000.

Clercq, Tanaquil Le. *The Ballet Cook Book*. New York: Stein and Day, Publishers, 1966.

Cooke, Alistair. *The Great and the Good*. New York: Arcade Publishing, 1999.

Crawford, John W. *Early Shakespearean Actresses*. New York: Peter Lang Publishing, Inc., 1984.

DeCaro, Frank. *A Boy Named Phyllis*. New York: Viking, 1996.

Deedy, John. *A Book of Catholic Anecdotes*. Allen, TX: Thomas More, 1997.

dePaola, Tomie. *Here We All Are*. New York: G.P. Putnam's Sons, 2000.

Domingo, Plácido. *My First Forty Years*. New York: Alfred A. Knopf, 1983.

Doonan, Simon. *Wacky Chicks: Life Lessons from Fearlessly Inappropriate and Fabulously Eccentric Women*. New York: Simon and Schuster, 2003.

Drennan, Robert E., editor. *The Algonquin Wits*. New York: The Citadel Press, 1968.

Drucker, Hal, and Sid Lerner. *From the Desk Of*. Photographs by Sing-Si Schwartz. San Diego, CA: Harcourt Brace Jovanovich, Publishers, 1989.

Eichenbaum, Rose. *Masters of Movement: Portraits of America's Great Choreographers*. Washington, D.C.: Smithsonian Books, 2004.

Ensler, Eve. *The Vagina Monologues*. New York: Villard Books, 2001.

Epstein, Lawrence J. *A Treasury of Jewish Anecdotes*. Northvale, NJ: Jason Aronson, Inc., 1989.

Erlanger, Ellen. *Jane Fonda: More Than a Movie Star*. Minneapolis, MN: Lerner Publications Company, 1984.

Feinberg, Morris "Moe." *Larry: The Stooge in the Middle*. San Francisco, CA: Last Gasp of San Francisco, 1984.

Ford, Carin T. *Legends of American Dance and Choreography*. Berkeley Heights, NJ: Enslow Publications, Inc., 2000.

Ford, Corey. *The Time of Laughter*. Boston, MA: Little, Brown and Company, 1967.

Foxx, Redd, and Norma Miller. *The Redd Foxx Encyclopedia of Black Humor*. Pasadena, CA: Ward Ritchie Press, 1977.

Freberg, Stan. *It Only Hurts When I Laugh*. New York: Times Books, 1988.

Fricke, Aaron. *Reflections of a Rock Lobster: A Story About Growing Up Gay*. Boston, MA: AlyCat Books, 1981.

Gielgud, John, and John Miller. *Acting Shakespeare*. New York: Charles Scribner's Sons, 1991.

Gielgud, John. *Distinguished Company*. London: Heinemann, 1972.

Goodman, Jack, and Albert Rice. *I Wish I'd Said That!* New York: Simon and Schuster, 1935.

Gordon, Mel. *The Seven Addictions and Five Professions of Anita Berber: Weimar Berlin's Priestess of Depravity*. Los Angeles, CA: Feral House, 2006.

Grody, Svetlana McLee, and Dorothy Daniels Lister. *Conversations With Choreographers*. Portsmouth, NH: Heinemann, 1996.

Grenfell, Joyce, et. al. *Joyce: By Herself and Her Friends*. London: Macdonald Futura Publishers, Limited, 1981.

Grenfell, Joyce. *Joyce Grenfell Requests the Pleasure*. London: Macdonald Futura Publishers, Ltd., 1976.

Groover, David L., and Cecil C. Conner, Jr. *Skeletons from the Opera Closet*. New York: St. Martin's Press, 1986.

Halliwell, Leslie. *The Filmgoer's Book of Quotes*. New Rochelle, NY: Arlington House Publishers, 1973.

Harris, Nick. *I Wish I'd Said That!* London: Octopus Books, Limited, 1984.

Hay, Peter. *Broadway Anecdotes*. New York: Oxford University Press, 1989.

Hecht, Ben. *Charlie: The Improbable Life and Times of Charles MacArthur*. New York: Harper & Brothers, Publishers, 1957.

Henry, Lewis C. *Humorous Anecdotes About Famous People*. Garden City, NY: Halcyon House, 1948.

Hewlett-Davies, Barry, editor and compiler. *A Night at the Opera*. New York: St. Martin's Press, 1980.

Holloway, Stanley. *Wiv a Little Bit O' Luck*. As told to Dick Richards. New York: Stein and Day, Publishers, 1967.

Huggett, Richard. *Supernatural on Stage: Ghosts and Superstitions of the Theatre*. New York: Taplinger Publishing Company, 1975.

Hughes, Holly. *Clit Notes: A Sapphic Sampler*. New York: Grove Press, 1996.

Javna, John. *The Best of TV Sitcoms*. New York: Harmony Books, 1988.

Jerome, Jerome K. *On the Stage — and Off: The Brief Career of a Would-Be Actor*. Wolfeboro Falls, NH: Alan Sutton Publishing, Inc., 1991.

Katkov, Norman. *The Fabulous Fanny*. New York: Alfred A. Knopf, 1953.

Laffey, Bruce. *Beatrice Lillie: The Funniest Woman in the World*. New York: Wynwood Press, 1989.

Leonard, Sheldon. *And the Show Goes On: Broadway and Hollywood Adventures*. New York: Limelight, 1994.

Levenson, Jill. *Shakespeare in Performance: Romeo and Juliet*. Wolfeboro, NH: Manchester University Press, 1987.

Levenson, Sam. *In One Era and Out the Other*. New York: Simon and Schuster, 1973.

Levine, Ellen. *Anna Pavlova: Genius of the Dance*. New York: Scholastic, Inc., 1995.

Linkletter, Art. *I Wish I'd Said That! My Favorite Ad-Libs of All Time*. Garden City, NY: Doubleday & Co., Inc., 1968.

Macnee, Patrick, and Marie Cameron. *Blind in One Ear: The Avenger Returns*. San Francisco, CA: Mercury House, Inc., 1989.

Maltin, Leonard. *Movie Comedy Teams*. New York: The New American Library, Inc., 1970.

Mankowitz, Wolf. *The ABC of Show Business*. London: Oldbourne Press, 1956.

Marinacci, Barbara. *Leading Ladies: A Gallery of Famous Actresses*. New York: Dodd, Mead and Company, 1961.

Marx, Arthur. *Son of Groucho*. New York: David McKay Company, Inc., 1972.

Marx, Samuel. *Broadway Portraits*. New York: Donald Flamm, Inc., 1929.

May, Robin, compiler. *The Wit of the Theatre*. London: Leslie Frewin, 1969.

McCann, Sean, compiler. *The Wit of Brendan Behan*. London: Leslie Frewin Publishers, Ltd., 1968.

Mendelsohn, S. Felix. *Here's a Good One: Stories of Jewish Wit and Wisdom*. New York: Block Publishing Co., 1947.

Meyer, Miriam Weiss, Project Editor. *Top Picks: People*. Pleasantville, NY: Reader's Digest Educational Division, 1977.

Midler, Bette. *A View from a Broad*. New York: Simon and Schuster, Inc., 1980.

Miller, Jeffrey S. *Something Completely Different: British Television and American Culture*. Minneapolis, MN: University of Minnesota Press, 2000.

Miller, John. *Judi Dench: With a Crack in Her Voice*. New York: Welcome Rain, Publishers, 2000.

Miller, John. *Ralph Richardson: The Authorized Biography*. London: Sidgwick and Jackson, 1995.

Moore, Grace. *You're Only Human Once*. Garden City, NY: Doubleday, Doran and Co., Inc., 1944.

Morley, Robert. *Around the World in Eighty-One Years*. London: Hodder & Stoughton, 1990.

Morley, Robert. *Robert Morley's Book of Bricks*. New York: G.P. Putnam's Sons, 1979.

Morrissey, James W. *Noted Men and Women*. New York: The Klebold Press, 1910.

Mostel, Kate, and Madeline Gilford. *170 Years of Show Business*. With Jack Gilford and Zero Mostel. New York: Random House, 1978.

Mostel, Zero, and Max Waldman. *Zero by Mostel*. New York: Horizon Press, 1965.

Nardo, Don. *Greek and Roman Theater*. San Diego, CA: Lucent Books, 1995.

Nicholson, Frank Ernest. *Favorite Jokes of Famous People*. New York: E.P. Dutton & Co., Inc., 1928.

Norkin, Sam. *Drawings, Stories: Theater, Opera, Ballet, Movies*. Portsmouth, NH: Heinemann, 1994.

Old, Wendie C. *Duke Ellington: Giant of Jazz*. Springfield, NJ: Enslow Publications, Inc., 1996.

Pearson, Hesketh. *Lives of the Wits*. New York: Harper and Row, Publishers, 1962.

Phillips, Julien. Stars of the Ziegfeld Follies. Minneapolis, MN: Lerner Publications Company, 1972.

Poley, Irvin C., and Ruth Verlenden Poley. *Friendly Anecdotes*. New York: Harper & Brothers, Publishers, 1950.

Pollack, Barbara, and Charles Humphrey Woodford. *Dance is a Moment: A Portrait of José Limón in Words and Pictures*. Pennington, NJ: Princeton Book Company, Publishers, 1993.

Powers, Tom. *Steven Spielberg: Master Storyteller*. Minneapolis, MN: Lerner Publications Company, 1997.

Price, Vincent. *The Book of Joe*. Garden City, NY: Doubleday & Co., Inc., 1961.

Primack, Ben, adapter and editor. *The Ben Hecht Show: Impolitic Observations from the Freest Thinker of 1950s Television*. Jefferson, NC: McFarland & Company, Inc., Publishers, 1993.

Richards, Dick, compiler. *The Wit of Noël Coward*. London: Leslie Frewin, 1968.

Richards, Dick, compiler. *The Wit of Peter Ustinov*. London: Leslie Frewin Publishers, Limited, 1969.

Rigg, Diana, compiler. *No Turn Unstoned: The Worst Ever Theatrical Reviews*. Los Angeles, CA: Silman-James Press, 1982.

Robinson, Simon. *A Year With Rudolf Nureyev*. With Derek Robinson. London: Robert Hale, Limited, 1997.

Rossi, Alfred. *Astonish Us in the Morning: Tyrone Guthrie Remembered*. London: Hutchinson and Co., Publishers, 1977.

Rosten, Leo. *People I Have Loved, Known or Admired*. New York: McGraw-Hill Book Company, 1970.

Russell, Mark, editor. *Out of Character*. New York: Bantam Books, 1997.

Rutkowska, Wanda. *Famous People in Anecdotes*. Warszawa: Wydawnictwa Szkolne i Pedagogiczne, 1977.

Rutter, Carol. *Clamorous Voices: Shakespeare's Women Today*. Edited by Faith Evans. New York: Routledge/Theatre Arts Books, 1989.

Sapieha, Virgilia, Ruth Neely, and Mary Love Collins. *Eminent Women: Recipients of the National Achievement Award*. Menasha, WI: George Banta Publishing Company, 1948.

Scheader, Catherine. *Lorraine Hansberry: Playwright and Voice of Justice*. Springfield, NJ: Enslow Publications, Inc., 1998.

Sessions, William H., collector. *More Quaker Laughter*. York, England: William Sessions, Limited, 1974.

Shindler, Phyllis, collector. *Raise Your Glasses*. London: Judy Piatkus, Limited, 1988.

Siddall, Stephen. *Cambridge Student Guide: Macbeth*. Cambridge: Cambridge University Press, 2002.

Silverman, Stephen M. *Funny Ladies: The Women Who Make Us Laugh*. New York: Harry N. Abrams, Inc., 1999.

Simons II, Minot. *Women's Gymnastics: A History. Volume 1: 1966 to 1974*. Carmel, CA: Welwyn Publishing Company, 1995.

Slide, Anthony. *Eccentrics of Comedy*. Lanham, Maryland, and London: The Scarecrow Press, Inc., 1998.

Smith, H. Allen. *The Life and Legend of Gene Fowler*. New York: William Morrow and Co., 1977.

Smith, Ira L. and H. Allen Smith. *Low and Inside*. Garden City, NY: Doubleday and Company, Inc., 1949.

Smith, O. *Recollections of O. Smith, Comedian*. New York: Theatre Library Association, 1979.

Sobol, Donald J., and Rose Sobol, *Encyclopedia Brown's Book of Strange But True Crimes*. New York: Scholastic, Inc., 1991.

Speaker-Yuan, Margaret. *Agnes de Mille*. New York: Chelsea House Publishers, 1990.

Stefoff, Rebecca. *Mary Tyler Moore: The Woman Behind the Smile*. New York: New American Library, 1986.

Stier, Theodore. *With Pavlova Around the World*. London: Hurst & Blackett, Ltd., 1927.

Sutherland, Douglas. *The English Gentleman's Mistress*. London: Debrett's Peerage, Limited, 1980.

Tanitch, Robert, deviser and compiler. *Ralph Richardson: A Tribute*. London: Evans Brothers, Limited, 1982.

Terry, Walter. *Ted Shawn: Father of American Dance*. New York: The Dial Press, 1976.

Tully, Jim. *A Dozen and One*. Hollywood: Murray & Gee, Inc., Publishers, 1943.

Turk, Ruth. *Lillian Hellman: Rebel Playwright*. Minneapolis, MN: Lerner Publications Company, 1995.

Unterbrink, Mary. *Funny Women: American Comediennes, 1860-1985*. Jefferson, NC: McFarland and Co., Inc., Publishers, 1987.

Wagenknecht, Edward. *Merely Players*. Norman, OK: University of Oklahoma Press, 1966.

Wallach, Eli. The *Good, the Bad, and Me: In My Anecdotage*. Orlando, FL: Harcourt, Inc., 2005.

Warren, Roz, editor. *Revolutionary Laughter: The World of Women Comics*. Freedom, CA: The Crossing Press, 1995.

Weintraub, Joseph, editor. T*he Wit and Wisdom of Mae West*. New York: G.P. Putnam's Sons, 1967.

White, Betty. *Here We Go Again: My Life in Television*. New York: St. Martin's Press, 1995.

Williams, Kenneth. *Acid Drops*. London: J.M. Dent & Sons, Ltd., 1980.

Woog, Adam. *Magicians and Illusionists*. San Diego, CA: Lucent Books, 2000.

Woolf, Vicki. *Dancing in the Vortex: The Story of Ida Rubinstein*. Australia: Harwood Academic Publishers, 2000.

Woollcott, Alexander. *Enchanted Aisles*. New York: G.P. Putnam's Sons, 1924.

Woollcott, Alexander. *Shouts and Murmurs: Echoes of a Thousand and One Nights*. New York: The Century Co., 1922.

Wright, David K. *Paul Robeson: Actor, Singer, Political Activist*. Berkeley Heights, NJ: Enslow Publications, Inc., 1998.

Youngman, Henny. *Take My Life, Please!* With Neal Karlen. New York: William Morris and Company, Inc., 1991.

Zolotow, Maurice. *No People Like Show People*. New York: Random House, 1951.

# Appendix B: About the Author

It was a dark and stormy night. Suddenly a cry rang out, and on a hot summer night in 1954, Josephine, wife of Carl Bruce, gave birth to a boy — me. Unfortunately, this young married couple allowed Reuben Saturday, Josephine's brother, to name their first-born. Reuben, aka "The Joker," decided that Bruce was a nice name, so he decided to name me Bruce Bruce. I have gone by my middle name — David — ever since.

Being named Bruce David Bruce hasn't been all bad. Bank tellers remember me very quickly, so I don't often have to show an ID. It can be fun in charades, also. When I was a counselor as a teenager at Camp Echoing Hills in Warsaw, Ohio, a fellow counselor gave the signs for "sounds like" and "two words," then she pointed to a bruise on her leg twice. Bruise Bruise? Oh yeah, Bruce Bruce is the answer!

Uncle Reuben, by the way, gave me a haircut when I was in kindergarten. He cut my hair short and shaved a small bald spot on the back of my head. My mother wouldn't let me go to school until the bald spot grew out again.

Of all my brothers and sisters (six in all), I am the only transplant to Athens, Ohio. I was born in Newark, Ohio, and have lived all around Southeastern Ohio. However, I moved to Athens to go to Ohio University and have never left.

At Ohio U, I never could make up my mind whether to major in English or Philosophy, so I got a bachelor's degree with a double major in both areas, then I added a master's degree in English and a master's degree in Philosophy.

Currently, and for a long time to come (I eat fruits and vegetables), I am spending my retirement writing books such as *Nadia Comaneci: Perfect 10*, *The Funniest People in Dance*, *Homer's* Iliad: *A Retelling in Prose*, and *William Shakespeare's* Macbeth: *A Retelling in Prose.*

If all goes well, I will publish one or two books a year for the rest of my life. (On the other hand, a good way to make God laugh is to tell Her your plans.)

By the way, my sister Brenda Kennedy writes romances such as *A New Beginning* and *Shattered Dreams.*

# Appendix C: Some Books by David Bruce

**Anecdote Collections**

*250 Anecdotes About Opera*

*250 Anecdotes About Religion*

*250 Anecdotes About Religion: Volume 2*

*250 Music Anecdotes*

*Be a Work of Art: 250 Anecdotes and Stories*

*The Coolest People in Art: 250 Anecdotes*

*The Coolest People in the Arts: 250 Anecdotes*

*The Coolest People in Books: 250 Anecdotes*

*The Coolest People in Comedy: 250 Anecdotes*

*Create, Then Take a Break: 250 Anecdotes*

*Don't Fear the Reaper: 250 Anecdotes*

*The Funniest People in Art: 250 Anecdotes*

*The Funniest People in Books: 250 Anecdotes*

*The Funniest People in Books, Volume 2: 250 Anecdotes*

*The Funniest People in Books, Volume 3: 250 Anecdotes*

*The Funniest People in Comedy: 250 Anecdotes*

*The Funniest People in Dance: 250 Anecdotes*

*The Funniest People in Families: 250 Anecdotes*

*The Funniest People in Families, Volume 2: 250 Anecdotes*

*The Funniest People in Families, Volume 3: 250 Anecdotes*

*The Funniest People in Families, Volume 4: 250 Anecdotes*

*The Funniest People in Families, Volume 5: 250 Anecdotes*

*The Funniest People in Families, Volume 6: 250 Anecdotes*

*The Funniest People in Movies: 250 Anecdotes*

*The Funniest People in Music: 250 Anecdotes*

*The Funniest People in Music, Volume 2: 250 Anecdotes*

*The Funniest People in Music, Volume 3: 250 Anecdotes*

*The Funniest People in Neighborhoods: 250 Anecdotes*

*The Funniest People in Relationships: 250 Anecdotes*

*The Funniest People in Sports: 250 Anecdotes*

*The Funniest People in Sports, Volume 2: 250 Anecdotes*

*The Funniest People in Television and Radio: 250 Anecdotes*

*The Funniest People in Theater: 250 Anecdotes*

*The Funniest People Who Live Life: 250 Anecdotes*
*The Funniest People Who Live Life, Volume 2: 250 Anecdotes*
*The Kindest People Who Do Good Deeds, Volume 1: 250 Anecdotes*
*The Kindest People Who Do Good Deeds, Volume 2: 250 Anecdotes*
*Maximum Cool: 250 Anecdotes*
*The Most Interesting People in Movies: 250 Anecdotes*
*The Most Interesting People in Politics and History: 250 Anecdotes*
*The Most Interesting People in Politics and History, Volume 2: 250 Anecdotes*
*The Most Interesting People in Politics and History, Volume 3: 250 Anecdotes*
*The Most Interesting People in Religion: 250 Anecdotes*
*The Most Interesting People in Sports: 250 Anecdotes*
*The Most Interesting People Who Live Life: 250 Anecdotes*
*The Most Interesting People Who Live Life, Volume 2: 250 Anecdotes*
*Reality is Fabulous: 250 Anecdotes and Stories*
*Resist Psychic Death: 250 Anecdotes*
*Seize the Day: 250 Anecdotes and Stories*

[1] Source: Eve Arden, *Three Phases of Eve*, p. 14.

[2] Source: Jeffrey S. Miller, *Something Completely Different*, p. 59.

[3] Source: Alfred Hickling, 'I was mugged by the movies.' *The Guardian*. 25 April 2007 <http://arts.guardian.co.uk/theatre/drama/story/0,,2064980,00.html>.

[4] Source: Nick Claussen, "Humorist returns to Athens with acclaimed one-woman show." *The Athens News*. 13 July 2006 <http://www.athensnews.com/index.php?action=viewarticle§ion=news&story_id=25423>.

[5] Source: a Lifetime *Intimate Portrait* program featuring Carol Burnett.

[6] Source: Lawrence J. Epstein, *A Treasury of Jewish Anecdotes*, p. 8.

[7] Source: Virgilia Sapieha, Ruth Neely, and Mary Love Collins, *Eminent Women: Recipients of the National Achievement Award*, pp. 75-76.

[8] Source: Tanaquil Le Clercq, *The Ballet Cook Book*, pp. 26-27.

[9] Source: Robert Morley, *Robert Morley's Book of Bricks*, pp. 92-93.

[10] Source: Minot Simons II, *Women's Gymnastics: A History. Volume 1: 1966 to 1974*, pp. 276, 278.

[11] Source: Tom Powers, *Steven Spielberg: Master Storyteller*, p. 94.

[12] Source: Patrick Macnee and Marie Cameron, *Blind in One Ear*, p. 140.

[13] Source: Barry Hewlett-Davies, *A Night at the Opera*, p. 20.

[14] Source: Hal Burton, editor, *Acting in the Sixties*, p. 36.

[15] Source: Nick Harris, *I Wish I'd Said That!*, p. 28.

[16] Source: Michèle Brown and Ann O'Connor, *Hammer and Tongues*, p. 155.

[17] Source: John Miller, *Ralph Richardson*, p. 280.

[18] Source: Alistair Cooke, *The Great and the Good*, p. 216.

[19] Source: Sarah Giles, *Fred Astaire: His Friends Talk*, p. 198.

[20] Source: Tanaquil Le Clercq, *The Ballet Cook Book*, pp. 23-24.

[21] Source: Henny Youngman, *Take My Life, Please!*, p. 153.

[22] Source: Joe E. Brown, *Laughter is a Wonderful Thing*, p. 209.

[23] Source: Tim Boxer, *The Jewish Celebrity Hall of Fame*, p. 290.

[24] Source: Eve Arden, *Three Faces of Eve*, p. 17.

[25] Source: O. Smith, *Recollections of O. Smith, Comedian*, pp. 14-15.

[26] Source: Theodore Stier, *With Pavlova Around the World*, p. 277.

[27] Source: John Miller, *Judi Dench: With a Crack in Her Voice*, p. 34.

[28] Source: O. Smith, *Recollections of O. Smith, Comedian*, p. xvi.

[29] Source: John Miller, *Ralph Richardson*, pp. xiv-xv.

[30] Source: Helen Caldwell, *Michio Ito: The Dancer and His Dances*, p. 164.

[31] Source: Maurice Zolotow, *No People Like Show People*, p. 184.

[32] Source: Susan Bivin Aller, *J.M. Barrie: The Magic Behind Peter Pan*, pp. 88-89.

[33] Source: Maurice Zolotow, *No People Like Show People*, p. 165.

[34] Source: Robin May, compiler, *The Wit of the Theatre*, p. 13.

[35] Source: Mark Russell, editor, *Out of Character*, p. 159.

[36] Source: Eli Wallach, *The Good, the Bad, and Me: In My Anecdotage*, p. 60.

[37] Source: Joyce Grenfell, et. al., *Joyce*, pp. 125-126.

[38] Source: Leonard Maltin, *Movie Comedy Teams*, p. 247.

[39] Source: Frank Ernest Nicholson, *Favorite Jokes of Famous People*, p. 124.

[40] Source: Adam Woog, *Magicians and Illusionists*, pp. 61-62.

[41] Source: Holly Hughes, *Clit Notes: A Sapphic Sampler*, p. 22.

[42] Source: Ellen Erlanger, *Jane Fonda: More Than a Movie Star*, p. 13.

[43] Source: Don Nardo, *Greek and Roman Theater*, p. 78.

[44] Source: Morris "Moe" Feinberg, *Larry: The Stooge in the Middle*, p. 55.

[45] Source: Leslie Halliwell, *The Filmgoer's Book of Quotes*, p. 16.

[46] Source: Eve Ensler, *The Vagina Monologues*, p. xxx.

[47] Source: Peter Hay, *Broadway Anecdotes*, pp. 232-233.

[48] Source: Mary Unterbrink, *Funny Women*, p. 38.

[49] Source: Don Nardo, *Greek and Roman Theater*, p. 74.

[50] Source: Sam Norkin, *Drawings, Stories*, pp. 12-13.

[51] Source: Tomie dePaola, *Here We All Are*, pp. 31-37.

[52] Source: John Gielgud and John Miller, *Acting Shakespeare*, pp. 64-65.

[53] Source: Richard Huggett, *Supernatural on Stage*, p. 174.

[54] Source: Miriam Weiss Meyer, project editor, *Top Picks: People*, p. 8.

[55] Source: Carin T. Ford, *Legends of American Dance and Choreography*, pp. 64, 68-69.

[56] Source: Alexander Woollcott, *Enchanted Aisles*, pp. 114-115.

[57] Source: Morwenna Banks and Amanda Swift, *The Joke's on Us*, pp. 108-109.

[58] Source: Ben Hecht, *Charlie: The Improbable Life and Times of Charles MacArthur*, p. 144.

[59] Source: Arthur Marx, *Son of Groucho*, p. 25.

[60] Source: Constance Benson, *Mainly Players*, p. 272.

[61] Source: Hal Burton, editor, *Acting in the Sixties*, p. 166.

[62] Source: Catherine Scheader, *Lorraine Hansberry: Playwright and Voice of Justice*, pp. 16-17.

[63] Source: Carol Rutter, *Clamorous Voices: Shakespeare's Women Today*, p. xxiii.

[64] Source: John W. Crawford, *Early Shakespearean Actresses*, p. 164.

[65] Source: Bette Midler, *A View from a Broad*, p. 44.

[66] Source: Julien Phillips, *Stars of the Ziegfeld Follies*, p. 21.

[67] Source: Nathaniel Benchley, *Robert Benchley*, pp. 151-153.

[68] Source: Ben Primack, adapter and editor, *The Ben Hecht Show*, p. 160.

[69] Source: Diana Rigg, compiler, *No Turn Unstoned*, pp. 8, 42, 114.

[70] Source: J. Bryan III, *Merry Gentlemen (and One Lady)*, pp. 45-46.

[71] Source: Franklin P. Adams, et. al., *Hammond: A Symposium in Tribute*, pp. 63-64.

[72] Source: Nathaniel Benchley, *Robert Benchley*, p. 172.

[73] Source: Joseph Weintraub, editor, *The Wit and Wisdom of Mae West*, p. 19.

[74] Source: Barbara Pollack and Charles Humphrey Woodford, *Dance is a Moment*, pp. 17-18.

[75] Source: Rose Eichenbaum, *Masters of Movement: Portraits of America's Great Choreographers*, pp. 190-191.

[76] Source: Simon Robinson, *A Year With Rudolf Nureyev*, p. 28.

[77] Source: Rose Eichenbaum, *Masters of Movement: Portraits of America's Great Choreographers*, p. 38.

[78] Source: Eli Wallach, *The Good, the Bad, and Me: In My Anecdotage*, p. 156.

[79] Source: Lewis C. Henry, *Humorous Anecdotes About Famous People*, p. 4.

[80] Source: David L. Groover and Cecil C. Conner, Jr., *Skeletons from the Opera Closet*, p. 14.

[81] Source: Jim Tully, *A Dozen and One*, p. 124.

[82] Source: Amy Allison, *Shakespeare's Globe*, p. 63.

[83] Source: Nick Harris, *I Wish I'd Said That!*, p. 69.

[84] Source: Corey Ford, *The Time of Laughter*, p. 60.

[85] Source: Svetlana McLee Grody and Dorothy Daniels Lister, *Conversations With Choreographers*, pp. 95, 102.

[86] Source: Robert Morley, *Around the World in Eighty-One Years*, p. 22.

[87] Source: Joey Adams, *The Borscht Belt*, pp. 16-17.

[88] Source: Joe E. Brown, *Laughter is a Wonderful Thing*, pp. 93-94.

[89] Source: Gyles Brandreth, *Great Theatrical Disasters*, p. 70.

[90] Source: Ellen Erlanger, *Jane Fonda: More Than a Movie Star*, pp. 15-16.

[91] Source: John Gielgud, *Distinguished Company*, p. 39.

[92] Source: Mark Russell, editor, *Out of Character*, p. 289.

[93] Source: Brian Logan, "Let's hear it for heroic failure." *The Times*. 11 June 2007 <http://entertainment.timesonline.co.uk/tol/arts_and_entertainment/stage/theatre/article1907811.ece>.

[94] Source: Sheldon Leonard, *And the Show Goes On*, p. 41.

[95] Source: Franklin P. Adams, et. al., *Percy Hammond: A Symposium in Tribute*, p. ix.

[96] Source: H. Allen Smith, *Life and Legend of Gene Fowler*, p. 12.

[97] Source: Robert Tanitch, deviser and compiler, *Ralph Richardson: A Tribute*, p. 90.

[98] Source: Morwenna Banks and Amanda Swift, *The Joke's on Us*, p. 116.

[99] Source: Constance Benson, *Mainly Players*, p. 75.

[100] Source: Peter Ustinov, writing in Wolf Mankowitz' *ABC of Show Business*, p. 3.

[101] Source: Bruce Laffey, *Beatrice Lillie*, p. 113.

[102] Source: Betty White, *Here We Go Again*, p. 175.

[103] Source: Alexander Woollcott, *Enchanted Aisles*, p. 245.

[104] Source: Alexander Woollcott, *Shouts and Murmurs*, p. 200.

[105] Source: Ruth Turk, *Lillian Hellman: Rebel Playwright*, pp. 51-52.

[106] Source: Frank DeCaro, *A Boy Named Phyllis*, p. 123.

[107] Source: Gyles Brandreth, *Great Theatrical Disasters*, p. 141.

[108] Source: Hal Drucker and Sid Lerner, *From the Desk Of*, p. 64.

[109] Source: Joyce Grenfell, *Joyce Grenfell Requests the Pleasure*, p. 148.

[110] Source: Antony Sher, "You don't have to be mad to be a great actor ... but it helps." *The Guardian*. 24 May 2007 <http://www.guardian.co.uk/g2/story/0,,2086640,00.html>.

[111] Source: Grace Moore, *You're Only Human Once*, p. 56.

[112] Source: Miriam Weiss Meyer, project editor, *Top Picks: People*, p. 7.

[113] Source: Jeremy Nichols, "Introduction" of Jerome K. Jerome's *On the Stage — and Off*, p. x.

[114] Source: Simon Doonan, *Wacky Chicks*, p. 105.

[115] Source: Catherine Scheader, *Lorraine Hansberry: Playwright and Voice of Justice*, p. 53.

[116] Source: John Miller, *Judi Dench: With a Crack in Her Voice*, p. 127.

[117] Source: David L. Groover and Cecil C. Conner, Jr., *Skeletons from the Opera Closet*, pp. 220-221.

[118] Source: Stan Freberg, *It Only Hurts When I Laugh*, pp. 145-146.

[119] Source: Paul Bailey, editor, *The Stately Homo: A Celebration of the Life of Quentin Crisp*, p. 240.

[120] Source: Barbara Marinacci, *Leading Ladies: A Gallery of Famous Actresses*, p. 91.

[121] Source: Jack Goodman and Albert Rice, *I Wish I'd Said That!*, p. 97.

[122] Source: Leo Rosten, *People I Have Loved, Known or Admired*, p. 88.

[123] Source: Barbara Marinacci, *Leading Ladies: A Gallery of Famous Actresses*, p. 42.

[124] Source: Wanda Rutkowska, *Famous People in Anecdotes*, p. 17.

[125] Source: Kenneth Williams, *Acid Drops*, pp. 89-90.

[126] Source: Dick Richards, compiler, *The Wit of Noël Coward*, p. 49.

[127] Source: Helen Caldwell, *Michio Ito: The Dancer and His Dances*, pp. 42, 44.

[128] Source: Bill Adler, *Jewish Wit and Wisdom*, p. 69.

[129] Source: John Burke, *Rogue's Progress: The Fabulous Adventures of Wilson Mizner*, pp. 14-15.

[130] Source: Joyce Grenfell, *Joyce Grenfell Requests the Pleasure*, pp. 202-203.

[131] Source: Frank Ernest Nicholson, *Favorite Jokes of Famous People*, p. 209.

[132] Source: Alistair Cooke, *The Great and the Good*, p. 216.

[133] Source: Ira L. Smith and H. Allen Smith, *Low and Inside*, pp. 29-30.

[134] Source: Alexander Woollcott, *Shouts and Murmurs*, p. 73.

[135] Source: Ellen Levine, *Anna Pavlova: Genius of the Dance*, pp. 70-71.

[136] Source: Vincent Price, *The Book of Joe*, pp. 95-96.

[137] Source: Wendie C. Old, *Duke Ellington: Giant of Jazz*, p. 60.

[138] Source: Walter Terry, *Ted Shawn: Father of American Dance*, pp. 115-116.

[139] Source: Sam Norkin, *Drawings, Stories*, p. 18.

[140] Source: Zero Mostel and Max Waldman, *Zero by Mostel*, unnumbered page in "Some Personal Words and Drawings."

[141] Source: John Gielgud and John Miller, *Acting Shakespeare*, p. 42.

[142] Source: John Gielgud, *Distinguished Company*, pp. 59-60.

[143] Source: Linda Winer, "Playwright Edward Albee celebrates his 80th year." 14 November 2007 <http://www.popmatters.com/pm/news/article/50964/playwright-edward-albee-celebrates-his-80th-year/>. This article originally appeared in *Newsday*.

[144] Source: Norman Katkov, *Fabulous Fanny*, p. 236.

[145] Source: Kate Mostel and Madeline Gilford, *170 Years of Show Business*, p. 74.

[146] Source: Stanley Holloway, *Wiv a Little Bit O' Luck*, p. 84.

[147] Source: Margaret Speaker-Yuan, *Agnes de Mille*, p. 40.

[148] Source: Robert Morley, *Robert Morley's Book of Bricks*, p. 8.

[149] Source: James W. Morrissey, *Noted Men and Women*, pp. 120ff.

[150] Source: Tim Boxer, *The Jewish Celebrity Hall of Fame*, p. 187.

[151] Source: Arthur Marx, *Son of Groucho*, p. 31.

[152] Source: Corey Ford, *The Time of Laughter*, p. 59.

[153] Source: Wendie C. Old, *Duke Ellington: Giant of Jazz*, pp. 47-48.

[154] Source: Alfred Rossi, *Astonish Us in the Morning*, pp. 190-191.

[155] Source: Ralph Berry, compiler and editor, *The Methuen Book of Shakespeare Anecdotes*, p. 100.

[156] Source: Samuel Marx, *Broadway Portraits*, p. 22.

[157] Source: Everett S. Allen, *Famous American Humorous Poets*, pp. 63, 65.

[158] Source: Sean McCann, compiler, *The Wit of Brendan Behan*, p. 63.

[159] Source: John Deedy, *A Book of Catholic Anecdotes*, pp. 25-26.

[160] Source: Plácido Domingo, *My First Forty Years*, pp. 66-67.

[161] Source: Michael Billington, "Taboo or not taboo?" *The Guardian*. 15 February 2007 <http://www.guardian.co.uk/g2/story/0,,2013254,00.html>.

[162] Source: Hesketh Pearson, *Lives of the Wits*, p. 99.

[163] Source: Wanda Rutkowska, *Famous People in Anecdotes*, pp. 62-63.

[164] Source: Jerome K. Jerome, *On the Stage — and Off*, pp. 64-65.

[165] Source: Redd Foxx and Norma Miller, *The Redd Foxx Encyclopedia of Black Humor*, pp. 159-160.

[166] Source: Theodore Stier, *With Pavlova Around the World*, pp. 278-279.

[167] Source: Stephen M. Silverman, *Funny Ladies*, p. 33.

[168] Source: Nancy Cartwright, *My Life as a 10-Year-Old Boy*, pp. 20-21.

[169] Source: J. Bryan III, *Merry Gentlemen (and One Lady)*, pp. 63-64.

[170] Source: Robert E. Drennan, editor, *The Algonquin Wits*, p. 148.

[171] Source: Paul Bailey, editor, *The Stately Homo: A Celebration of the Life of Quentin Crisp*, p. 217.

[172] Source: Brenda Wilkinson, *African American Women Writers*, p. 93.

[173] Source: Peter Hay, *Broadway Anecdotes*, p. 244.

[174] Source: S. Felix Mendelsohn, *Here's a Good One*, p. 205.

[175] Source: Eddie Cantor, *As I Remember Them*, p. 50.

[176] Source: Robert E. Drennan, editor, *The Algonquin Wits*, pp. 90-91.

[177] Source: David K. Wright, *Paul Robeson: Actor, Singer, Political Activist*, pp. 79, 113.

[178] Source: Donald J. Sobol and Rose Sobol, *Encyclopedia Brown's Book of Strange But True Crimes*, pp. 76-77.

[179] Source: Ira L. Smith and H. Allen Smith, *Low and Inside*, pp. 232-233.

[180] Source: John W. Crawford, *Early Shakespearean Actresses*, p. 67.

[181] Source: Amy Allison, *Shakespeare's Globe*, pp. 15-16, 45.

[182] Source: Ben Primack, adapter and editor, *The Ben Hecht Show*, pp. 136-137.

[183] Source: Simon Robinson, *A Year With Rudolf Nureyev*, p. 31.

[184] Source: John Burke, *Rogue's Progress: The Fabulous Adventures of Wilson Mizner*, p. 98.

[185] Source: Mel Gordon, *The Seven Addictions and Five Professions of Anita Berber*, p. 42.

[186] Source: Ellen Levine, *Anna Pavlova: Genius of the Dance*, p. 71.

[187] Source: Ruth Turk, *Lillian Hellman: Rebel Playwright*, pp. 88-89.

[188] Source: Jeffrey Zaslow, "Straight Talk," *USA Weekend*, Dec. 26-28, 1997.

[189] Source: Robert Tanitch, deviser and compiler, *Ralph Richardson: A Tribute*, p. 89.

[190] Source: Anthony Slide, *Eccentrics of Comedy*, p. 30.

[191] Source: Leslie Halliwell, *The Filmgoer's Book of Quotes*, Foreword.

[192] Source: Joseph Weintraub, editor, *The Wit and Wisdom of Mae West*, p. 19.

[193] Source: Alfred Rossi, *Astonish Us in the Morning*, p. 204.

[194] Source: Dick Richards, compiler, *The Wit of Noël Coward*, p. 28.

[195] Source: Irvin C. Poley and Ruth Verlenden Poley, *Friendly Anecdotes*, p. 68.

[196] Source: William H. Sessions, collector, *More Quaker Laughter*, p. 100.

[197] Source: Aaron Fricke, *Reflections of a Rock Lobster: A Story About Growing Up Gay*, p. 52.

[198] Source: Dick Richards, compiler, *The Wit of Peter Ustinov*, pp. 18-19.

[199] Source: Eve Ensler, *The Vagina Monologues*, p. 154. Of course, Ms. Ensler did not use asterisks. (The author of the book you are reading is a w*mp.)

[200] Source: Ben Hecht, *Charlie: The Improbable Life and Times of Charles MacArthur*, p. 93.

[201] Source: Lawrence J. Epstein, *A Treasury of Jewish Anecdotes*, pp. 125-126.

[202] Source: Stan Freberg, *It Only Hurts When I Laugh*, pp. 254-255.

[203] Source: Richard Huggett, *Supernatural on Stage*, p. 211.

[204] Source: Susan Bivin Aller, *J.M. Barrie: The Magic Behind Peter Pan*, pp. 116-117, 199.

[205] Source: Stephen M. Silverman, *Funny Ladies*, p. 59.

[206] Source: Grace Moore, *You're Only Human Once*, p. 47.

[207] Source: Kenneth Williams, *Acid Drops*, p. 7.

[208] Source: Holly Hughes, *Clit Notes: A Sapphic Sampler*, pp. 16, 113-114.

[209] Source: Art Linkletter, *I Wish I'd Said That!*, p. 113.

[210] Source: Kate Mostel and Madeline Gilford, *170 Years of Show Business*, p. 39.

[211] Source: Douglas Sutherland, *The English Gentleman's Mistress*, p. 20.

[212] Source: Robin May, compiler, *The Wit of the Theatre*, p. 90.

[213] Source: Vicki Woolf, *Dancing in the Vortex: The Story of Ida Rubinstein*, pp. 37-38.

[214] Source: Patrick Macnee and Marie Cameron, *Blind in One Ear*, pp. 87-89.

[215] Source: Ralph Berry, compiler and editor, *The Methuen Book of Shakespeare Anecdotes*, p. 105.

[216] Source: Stephen Siddall, *Cambridge Student Guide:* Macbeth, p. 104.

[217] Source: Phyllis Shindler, collector, *Raise Your Glasses*, p. 93.

[218] Source: Carol Rutter, *Clamorous Voices: Shakespeare's Women Today*, pp. xvi-xvii.

[219] Source: Edward Wagenknecht, *Merely Players*, p. 165.

[220] Source: Jill Levenson, *Shakespeare in Performance:* Romeo and Juliet, p. 100.

[221] Source: Roz Warren, editor, *Revolutionary Laughter*, p. 72.

[222] Source: Anthony Slide, *Eccentrics of Comedy*, p. 32.

[223] Source: Edward Wagenknecht, *Merely Players*, p. 132.

[224] Source: David K. Wright, *Paul Robeson: Actor, Singer, Political Activist*, p. 17.

[225] Source: John Javna, *The Best of TV Sitcoms*, p. 52.

[226] Source: Diana Rigg, compiler, *No Turn Unstoned*, p. 39.

[227] Source: Joey Adams, *The Borscht Belt*, p. 77.

[228] Source: Walter Terry, *Ted Shawn: Father of American Dance*, p. 141.

[229] Source: Eddie Cantor, *As I Remember Them*, p. 35.

[230] Source: Rebecca Stefoff, *Mary Tyler Moore: The Woman Behind the Smile*, p. 155.

[231] Source: Julien Phillips, *Stars of the Ziegfeld Follies*, p. 25.

[232] Source: Bruce Laffey, *Beatrice Lillie*, p. 205.

[233] Source: Michèle Brown and Ann O'Connor, *Hammer and Tongues*, p. 99.

[234] Source: Virgilia Sapieha, Ruth Neely, and Mary Love Collins, *Eminent Women: Recipients of the National Achievement Award*, p. 96.

[235] Source: Art Linkletter, *I Wish I'd Said That!*, pp. 26-27.

[236] Source: Barry Hewlett-Davies, *A Night at the Opera*, p. 143.

[237] Source: Ralph Berry, *On Directing Shakespeare*, p. 207.

[238] Source: Norman Katkov, *Fabulous Fanny*, p. 44.

[239] Source: David Brown, *Star Billing: Tell-Tale Trivia from Hollywood*, pp. 18-19.

[240] Source: Carin T. Ford, *Legends of American Dance and Choreography*, pp. 55-57, 59.

[241] Source: Joyce Grenfell, *Joyce Grenfell Requests the Pleasure*, pp. 114-115.

[242] Source: Stanley Holloway, *Wiv a Little Bit O' Luck*, p. 218.

[243] Source: Svetlana McLee Grody and Dorothy Daniels Lister, *Conversations With Choreographers*, p. 147.

[244] Source: Lewis C. Henry, *Humorous Anecdotes About Famous People*, p. 7.

[245] Source: Sheldon Leonard, *And the Show Goes On*, p. 205.

[246] Source: Samuel Marx, *Broadway Portraits*, p. 20.

[247] Source: Sean McCann, compiler, *The Wit of Brendan Behan*, pp. 64-65.

[248] Source: Hesketh Pearson, *Lives of the Wits*, p. 92.

[249] Source: Jim Tully, *A Dozen and One*, p. 130.

[250] Source: Sam Levenson, *In One Era and Out the Other*, p. 22.